The Captives; or, the Lost Recovered.

THE
CAPTIVES;
OR,
The Lost Recovered.

Written by Thomas Heywood.

Edited, with Introduction, Notes, & Glossary,
By ALEXANDER CORBIN JUDSON,
Associate Professor of English in the University of Texas.

NEW HAVEN:
Printed for and published by the Yale University Press.
London: Humphrey Milford: Oxford University Press.
MDCCCCXXI

Published Under the Auspices of the
ELIZABETHAN CLUB
YALE UNIVERSITY
In Memory of
FRANCIS BERGEN
of the Class of 1914, *Yale College.*

THE *present volume is the first work published in memory of Francis Bergen, under the auspices of the Elizabethan Club, of which he was an honored member. He was born in Montclair, New Jersey, on January 30, 1892, and graduated from Yale College in the Class of 1914. While an undergraduate at Yale he contributed articles to many of the college periodicals, served on the editorial board of the* Yale Literary Magazine, *and was one of the recognized leaders in his class. After graduation he was entered at New College, Oxford, for a post-graduate course, but was prevented from taking up his work there by the outbreak of the war. He accordingly entered the Harvard Law School in the autumn of 1914, and as a Senior was, at the time of his death, entitled to the degree of LL.B. without examination, having enlisted for active military service. For this he had prepared himself by spending the summers of 1915 and 1916 at Plattsburg, serving in the year last mentioned with a machine gun troop of the regular army then stationed there. He was killed May 11, 1917, by the overturn of the automobile in which he was again going to Plattsburg to enter the Reserve Officers' Training Camp, established after the decision of the United States to bear its part in the Great War. In his memory, his father, in May, 1919, established, at Yale, a foundation for the delivery of the Francis Bergen Lectures each year on Recent English Poetry, Recent English Prose Literature, Recent Dramatic Literature and Drama, and Recent Advances and Achievements in Science.*

CONTENTS

PREFACE

THE Captives; or, The Lost Recovered" is the only play now generally ascribed to Thomas Heywood which is not contained in the standard edition of his dramatic works, published by John Pearson in 1874. Its omission was due to the fact that it had not at that time been discovered. In 1885 Mr. A. H. Bullen, who had shortly before stumbled upon it in a British Museum manuscript, printed it in the fourth volume of his "Collection of Old English Plays." Unfortunately the edition was limited to one hundred and fifty copies, and apparently not many of these have found their way to America. It was mainly with the purpose of making "The Captives" more generally accessible that the present edition was undertaken. The play deserves more attention than it has received. Professor Philipp Aronstein, perhaps Heywood's most able critic, says of it: "Heywood is always, above everything else, a theatrical craftsman. But this play is, moreover, distinguished by the harmony and the charming tenderness and grace of Heywood's best art."*

Mr. Jeayes, of the Manuscript Department of the British Museum, and Mr. Bullen made the initial transcription of the manuscript. I have, with considerable care, collated Mr. Bullen's edition with rotographs of the manuscript, a labor which has justified itself. I have been able to include several passages which Mr. Bullen found himself unable to read, and, aside from mere changes in spelling and punctuation, have altered his readings at a number of points. All important departures from the text in the Bullen edition have been indicated in the foot-notes. In a semi-popular

*Anglia 37. 257.

edition like the present, one might expect a complete modern-
izing of the text. I have, however, retained the spelling of the
manuscript, because my verbal departures from the only other
printed version suggested the desirability of as faithful a repro-
duction of the original as possible. In general, I have striven for
brevity in the critical apparatus, though I have treated the matter of sources with some fullness because of the peculiarly good
opportunity offered for the study of Heywood's characteristic
handling of source material.

To those who have aided me in the preparation of this edition
my hearty thanks are due, especially to my colleague, Professor
Robert A. Law, who has read all the proof sheets and given me
valuable suggestions.

A. C. JUDSON.

INTRODUCTION

Authorship of "The Captives."

ALTHOUGH the manuscript of "The Captives" does not bear Heywood's name, there is ample evidence that Heywood is the author. The internal evidence alone is sufficient to satisfy the average student of the Elizabethan drama. The metrical characteristics of the verse, the nature of the domestic scenes involving the Lord and the Lady of Averne, the type of humor furnished by the clown, the peculiar grace and gentleness of conduct revealed by Raphael and the Lady of Averne—all these stamp the play as Heywood's. It is not, however, necessary to depend on internal evidence alone. The "MS. Office-Book" of Sir Henry Herbert has, under the date of September 3, 1624, the following entry: "For the Cockpit Company;* A new Play, called, *The Captive, or the Lost recovered:* Written by Hayward."† Though the manuscript is without title, there seems no reason to doubt that this is the play referred to. A further bit of evidence is furnished by Mr. Bullen, who calls attention to the fact that "The Captives" and "Calisto," the piece, consisting of scenes from Heywood's "Golden Age" and "Silver Age," that immediately follows, are written in the same very striking hand, which appears nowhere else in the volume.‡ As far as I am aware, Heywood's authorship of "The Captives" has not seriously been questioned by any critic.

*Probably the Lady Elizabeth's Company.— Murray, "English Dramatic Companies" 1.259.

†Adams, "Dramatic Records of Sir Henry Herbert," p. 29.

‡"Collection of Old English Plays" 2.419.

Date of "The Captives."

THE entry from Sir Henry Herbert's "Office-Book," quoted above, which informs us that "The Captives" was licensed September 3, 1624, furnishes what is, without much question, approximately the date of composition of the play. Even were Sir Henry Herbert's entry lacking, one would still be safe in assigning the play to about this time on account of its metrical characteristics. Metrically, "The Captives" corresponds more nearly than does any other play of Heywood's to "The English Traveler," which seems to have been first acted during or not long after 1625.* In these two plays, Heywood employs most consistently various devices—numerous run-on lines, many feminine endings, many short and broken lines, and next to no rhyme—for securing a natural, easy vehicle for his dialogue, which approaches at times almost the effect of prose. Very few of Heywood's plays can be so accurately and certainly dated.

Egerton MS. 1994 and Mr. Bullen's Edition.

THERE has been hitherto but one edition of "The Captives," that of Mr. A. H. Bullen, contained in Volume IV of his work entitled "A Collection of Old English Plays," privately printed by Wyman & Sons, Great Queen Street, Lincoln's-Inn Fields, London, 1885. Until its publication the play was preserved in a single manuscript (Egerton MS. 1994), purchased by the British Museum at Lord Charlemont's sale, August 6, 1865. The history of the manuscript prior to this date is unknown.

A hasty examination of the manuscript reveals forty-three large pages, written in a rapid hand very unlike that found in most state letters and other documents of the time. Corrections, varying from the alteration of a single word to the marking for omis-

*See Aronstein, *Anglia* 37.239.

sion of a score or more of lines, appear on almost every page. The edges of some of the leaves are slightly blurred and torn, but surprisingly few words have been rendered illegible.

A closer examination reveals a number of marginal notes, made perhaps by some theatrical manager. These call attention to the point at which various characters soon to appear must be warned, mention stage-paraphernalia needed, and indicate more clearly entrances and exits. At several points the names of certain of the actors—Gibson, Jack, and Taylor—have been written in the margin, but elsewhere the actors are referred to by their play-names. Not only is the handwriting in the margin different from the rest, but one word appears in it consistently with different spelling: *John* in the marginal notes, *Jhon* throughout the text.

A careful study of the manuscript has convinced me that it is autograph. Again and again occur corrections and alterations that only an author would be likely to make. In the foot-notes to the text, the more significant verbal corrections have been recorded; most of these are quite evidently in the same hand as the body of the play, and some were made before the lines in which they occur were completed. Often the reason for the change is apparent. For example, line 14, scene 3, act 2, ends with *sinnes*, which is immediately preceded by *vill*, scored through. Evidently Heywood's intention was to end the line with *villainies*, but realizing when he had written the first syllable that he was about to spoil the metre, he crossed out *vill*, and wrote *sinnes* after it. In the elimination of certain lines, too, we can see the mind of Heywood at work. In 2.1.14-17 Palestra thus speaks of the procurer Mildew, who she imagines has been drowned:

> What shall I thinke
> Becoms of my base guardien? Though the waves
> Have spared the guiltles, suer his putrid soule
> Canot escape heaven's justyce!

But between the third and fourth lines occur these deleted lines:

> Is, if there be left any mercy for him,
> Nowe in these bryny waves made cleane for heaven.*

After Heywood had written them, he evidently felt that he was causing Palestra to speak too mildly of her "base guardien," and so drew his pen through them, and wrote in their place the words, "Canot escape heaven's justyce." Another illustration is found at 4.2.62. Here occur two lines that have been canceled. The reason for their elimination not being clear, I was tempted to restore them to the text till I discovered two lines almost word for word the same, thirty-three lines further on in the scene. Heywood apparently preferred to use them at their second occurrence, and so crossed them out where they had first been written. The canceled passage will be found in a note on 4.2.62. After becoming convinced that we have "The Captives" in Heywood's own hand, I was informed by Mr. J. P. Gilson, Keeper of the Manuscripts and Egerton Librarian in the British Museum, that the British Museum has nothing in Heywood's hand apart from this manuscript, and that he believes the identification of the handwriting must rest on internal evidence. He added, however, that "the catalogue made the suggestion (while the authorship was still unidentified) that the play was autograph."

While it seems clear that Heywood is responsible for certain deleted lines in the manuscript, there are other lines, and even passages of some length, that may have been marked for omission by another. The purpose was apparently to shorten individual speeches that lagged, or perhaps to reduce the length of the play as a whole, though all the lines so marked total but 223.† These lines will be printed as a part of the text, as in Mr. Bullen's edition, and indicated in the foot-notes.

---

*There are really three lines, but, as the second seems to be an exact repetition of the first in more legible form, only the second and the third need to concern us.

†Cf., for example, 1.1.5-27; 2.1.8-32; 3.2.130-139.

In his preface (page v), Mr. Bullen thus comments upon the difficulties of transcription: "Mr. Jeayes, of the Manuscript Department of the British Museum, undertook the labor of transcription and persevered to the end. As I have elsewhere stated, the play is written in a detestable hand; and few can appreciate the immense trouble that it cost Mr. Jeayes to make his transcript. Where Mr. Jeayes' labor ended, mine began; I spent many days in minutely comparing the transcript with the original. There are still left passages that neither of us could decipher, but they are not numerous." Mr. Bullen has attempted in his edition to follow the manuscript accurately as far as spelling goes, but has modernized the punctuation. He has also provided foot-notes, which define a number of archaic and obsolete words, call attention to several of the closest imitations of "Rudens," and note most of the passages that have been scored through or marked for omission. Though later editors may point out flaws in Mr. Bullen's text, they must remain deeply indebted to him for discovering the manuscript, and for superintending the initial transcript of its extraordinarily difficult hand.

Sources.

"THE CAPTIVES," like many of Heywood's plays, has a double plot. In the main plot, Palestra and Scribonia, two beautiful and pure maidens, escape from the control of Mildew, a procurer, are befriended by John Ashburne, an English merchant of Marseilles, and are finally discovered, through a cabinet long in Mildew's possession, to be Ashburne's daughter and niece respectively, kidnapped as babies. In the underplot the Duke of Averne kills a friar who has made advances to his wife, and so disposes of the body that it appears a brother friar has committed the murder, but at the last he saves the guiltless friar by confessing his deed. The connection between the two plots is slight, being practically confined to Palestra and Scribonia's seeking refuge with the friars after the escape from Mildew.

The main plot, which constitutes considerably more than two-thirds of the play, is derived from Plautus' comedy "Rudens."* Heywood has followed his original closely as regards both the characters† and the general progress of the action. Yet out of the 2000 lines that concern themselves chiefly with this plot, only about 350 represent a close verbal paralleling of his original.

Most of the passages from "Rudens" that have been imitated so closely as to make a detailed comparison interesting will be found, as they occur, in the notes. Though Heywood faithfully preserves the general situation and sequence of events in the original, he expands and reduces the matter, and alters details, as his taste dictates. Passages comprising about 350 lines of the main plot are entirely original with Heywood. These additions

* See A. H. Gilbert, "Thomas Heywood's Debt to Plautus," *Journal of English and Germanic Philology* 12. 593-611, for Heywood's use of Plautus in other plays as well as in "The Captives."

Dr. A. H. Ward, in his chapter on Heywood in "The Cambridge History of English Literature" (6.116), says in reference to "The Captives": "The main story is taken from the 'Rudens' of Plautus, several passages in which are translated in the play, but it seems to have reached the author through the Italian hand of Masuccio Salernitano." Dr. Ward must be thinking of the underplot, which Heywood derived from a *novella* of Masuccio di Salerno. See page 17.

† Every one of the important characters in "Rudens" finds a counterpart in "The Captives." Dæmones, an aged Athenian now living at Cyrene, reappears as Ashburne, an English merchant now living at Marseilles; Plesidippus, a young Athenian in love with Palæstra, as Raphael, a young merchant of Marseilles, in love with Palestra; Sceparnio, servant of Dæmones, as Godfrey, servant of Ashburne; Gripus, servant of Dæmones, as the Fisherman, or Gripus, servant of Ashburne; Trachalio, servant of Plesidippus, as the Clown, servant of Raphael; Labrax, a procurer, as Mildew, a procurer; Charmides, a Sicilian, his guest, as Sarleboys, his guest and friend; Palæstra and Ampelisca, young women in the possession of Labrax, as Palestra and Scribonia, young women in the possession of Mildew. Ptolemocratia, priestess of Venus, fills a function similar to that of the Abbot.

consist mainly of songs, scenes required to give points of contact
between the two plots, and a concluding scene in which the Elizabethan play-goer was enabled to learn how things turned out.
At no point does Heywood give one the impression of being
mastered, or even hampered, by his sources.

In the adaptation of his classical story to modern times, Heywood has not been altogether successful. The action of his drama
is represented as taking place about 1550* in France, and yet a
slave purchases his liberty from an English master, a procurer
plies his trade openly, and a young gentleman buys his wife for
three hundred crowns. That Heywood recognized the desirability of some changes in order to fit his story to sixteenth-cen-
tury France is apparent from certain changes, both major and
minor, that he has made. The temple of Venus, presided over
by a priestess of Venus, where the two girls ask for protection,
becomes a monastery in charge of a high-minded abbot; the sacred pitcher which Ampelisca carries as she goes for water becomes in the hands of Scribonia a pail with the name of the monastery engraved upon it; Palestra's casket contains not the Ro-
man trinkets—the little golden sword and axe and the little silver knife—but embroidered handkerchiefs and her baby-clothes.
Heywood's failure more thoroughly to adapt his matter to the
requirements of the new time and place may be explained partly
by the general uncritical character of his age, and partly by his
own peculiarly naïve outlook. Such incongruities as those mentioned above would not be likely much to disturb one who could
calmly distort life as it is distorted in "The Four Prentices" or
"The Fair Maid of the West."

On the other hand, Heywood has, at least in the opinion of
modern readers, improved in some respects upon his original.

*In 4.1.305, "1600" was originally given as the date of Palestra's birth, but this
has been corrected in the MS. to read "1530."

Though "Rudens" is by no means a monotonous play, it contains certain scenes that seem drawn out to a needless length. Heywood, while preserving rather faithfully the successive situations found in no fewer than thirty-two scenes in "Rudens," reduces considerably the longer conversations, and secures variety by the introduction of an echo-scene,* in which Palestra's pleas for succor seem to reverberate in the comfortless responses of Friar John, by Gripus' song in praise of poverty,† and by Palestra's and Mildew's song at the time of the maidens' recapture.‡ Thus this play reveals one of Heywood's most striking traits, his passion for variety. More notable is his addition of a scene presenting a satisfactory dénouement. At least one critic has called attention to the abruptness of Plautus' ending. Sceparnio, Dæmones' clever servant, does not reappear in the latter part of the play, Plesidippus and Palæstra are not reunited, we do not know what becomes of Ampelisca, and the play closes flatly with Dæmones inviting Gripus and the procurer to dine with him. Not so with Heywood. His readers must know the outcome, and in this case at least it must be a very cheerful outcome, possibly to balance the tragic note in the sub-plot. And so Treadway, a character apparently introduced expressly for the purpose, wins the hand of Scribonia, who turns out to be Ashburne's niece; Raphael, Heywood's substitute for Plesidippus, is joined once more to Palestra; and Ashburne, who takes the place of Dæmones, is informed through the arrival of his brother from England that his enemies are dead, and that a large estate has been left to him. Finally, Heywood is able to sound his familiar note of patriotism as he turns the faces of his exiles toward England. Some may feel that the conclusion is altogether too satisfactory—that in it Heywood has done too great violence to probability. Yet no one can fail to value the completeness and sense of unity that it gives. Besides

*2.1.88 ff.   †4.1.417-444.   ‡3.2.46-61.

the alterations just enumerated, Heywood has modified his material by a rather subtle change in atmosphere. His humanity, which makes him the most lovable of the Elizabethan dramatists, appears again and again. It is evident, for example, in Raphael's attitude toward Palestra. It reveals itself still more clearly in the character of Ashburne, the old merchant whose heart has never ceased to yearn for his daughter; Ashburne possesses a dignity and fineness of character quite lacking in Dæmones. This change in atmosphere is perhaps the most welcome of Heywood's changes.

The secondary plot of "The Captives" shows about the same degree of originality as the main plot. Its source, as Professor Emil Koeppel pointed out in 1896,* is to be found in a *novella* of Masuccio di Salerno. The *novella* from which Heywood derived his story is the first of fifty brief narratives printed at Naples in 1476 under the title "Novellino." Their favorite theme is priestly immorality; and the whole collection is written with so much vigor and originality that it is easy to understand the popularity that they long enjoyed.

Oddly enough, Professor Koeppel's discovery of the source of the underplot seems to have been overlooked by recent students of the drama. In 1898, Professor Kittredge printed a note on "The Captives"† in which he remarked that the "underplot is merely a version of the well-known Old French *fabliau* of 'Le Prêtre qu'on porte,' already represented in English by the 'Mery Jest of Dan Hew of Leicestre.'"‡ Professor Kittredge's note apparently furnishes the basis for what Dr. Ward has to say on the subject in the "Cambridge History of English Literature,"|| and is admittedly the basis of Professor Schelling's brief statement

---

Archiv für das Studium der Neueren Sprachen und Litteraturen 97.323-329.
† *Journal of Germanic Philology* 2.13.
‡Hazlitt, "Early Popular Poetry of England" 3.133-146. ||6.116.

in his "Elizabethan Drama."* Professor Aronstein, in his comprehensive study of Heywood in *Anglia†* alludes to Professor Koeppel's article, but implies that the Dan Hew story is now recognized to be Heywood's more immediate source. The Old French *fabliau* referred to by Professor Kittredge appears in at least three distinct versions, entitled respectively: "Du Segretain ou du Moine,"‡ "Du Segretain Moine,"|| and "Le Dit dou Soucretain."§ Though they all differ in various minor details, all contain the same series of events.¶ The "Mery Jest of Dane Hew, Munk of Leicester," alluded to by Professor Kittredge, is merely another version of the same tale. In the crude but vigorous verse of the jest-book, we are told how Dan Hew suffered death no less than five times. The story opens with the monk's efforts to win to his desires a certain woman good and fair, the wife of a tailor. When he persists in spite of her refusal, she finally agrees to receive him on the next day, after her husband has ridden out of town, provided he pays her twenty nobles. The monk, on his arrival, is told to place the money in a chest, from which her husband, who has been concealed within, immediately springs out and kills him. The husband then carries the monk's body to the abbey, and sets it up against the wall. Soon the abbot comes upon Dan Hew, addresses him, gets no response, and strikes him with a staff. At once, under the impression that he has killed him, he has the body conveyed back and set upright at the tailor's door. The tailor later finds him there, and fearing that he may still be alive, strikes him down

*1.352. †37.255.

‡Montaiglon et Raynaud, "Recueil Général" 5.115-131 (CXXIII).

||*Ibid.* 5.215-242 (CXXXVI). §*Ibid.* 6.117-137 (CL).

¶Other references to the *fabliaux* in the "Recueil Général," given by Joseph Bédier in his "Les Fabliaux," page 469, under the heading "Le prêtre qu'on porte," and quoted by Professor Kittredge in the *Journal of Germanic Philology* (2.13), have little or no connection with the tale under consideration.

with his poleax. The next morning he bears the corpse away in a sack, with the intention of throwing it into the mill-pond, but, chancing upon a sack of bacon temporarily abandoned by some thieves, he substitutes the body for the bacon. When the thieves discover his trick, they bring back the body, and hang it up beside the mill, on the very hook from which they had stolen the bacon. The miller, aghast at the body, conceives the idea of strapping it, with a long pole in its hand, upon a stallion belonging to the abbot, in the hope that it may appear to pursue the abbot on the following morning when he rides forth on his mare. This plan succeeds, and the abbot in terror cries out that Dan Hew is trying to get his revenge. The abbot's men then rush out, and strike the body to the earth. The poem closes with the following lines:

> So they killed him once again,
> Thus was he once hanged, and foure times slaine,
> And buried at the last, as it was best.
> I pray God send vs all good rest.

This summary of the "Mery Jest of Dane Hew" gives a good idea of the *fabliaux*. They are naturally very like the jest-book tale in general tone; and in their action but two variations worth mentioning occur—the monk is set up in a privy in all three of the French versions instead of against a wall, and at the end he is bound upon a colt (*poulain*) instead of upon a stallion, and the pursuit of the abbot on his mare does not take place. Evidently the relationship between all these tales is very close. But between these tales and Heywood's underplot there exists a most fundamental difference. From Heywood's plot the entire incident connected with the substitution of the monk's body for the bacon is lacking, and accordingly, with Heywood, it is the aggrieved husband who finally places the body upon the horse, not the owner of the bacon. Many less fundamental differences also occur, as, for example, the absence from Heywood's version of the motive of gain on the part of the wife, which prompts her to encourage Dan Hew's fatal visit. That a relationship exists between the Dan Hew story, with its French counterparts, and the underplot of "The Captives" is perfectly obvious, but no one who will compare them with the summary of Masuccio's novel given below will have the slightest question as to which Heywood is more likely to have employed.

A certain friar named Maestro Diego da Revalo, comely in person and noted for his learning, was attached to a religious house in Salamanca. One day, while preaching, his eye fell upon a young lady of marvelous beauty, the wife of one of the chief gentlemen of the city, Messer Roderico d'Angiaja, and he immediately conceived a passionate love for her. Accordingly, after turning the matter over in his mind, he wrote a letter that set forth with great fullness the state of his heart, and sent it to her. She was pleased at the praise of her beauty, but, having no fondness for friars, returned him an unsympathetic answer. Nothing daunted, he continued to importune her, so that she could not look out of her window or enter the church without seeing him hovering near. So noticeable became his attentions that she began to fear for her good name, and laid the whole matter before her husband. His rage was such that he was tempted to carry fire and sword at once against the convent; however, calming his anger, he bade his wife invite Maestro Diego to his house the following night, but to leave other plans to him. Though it was difficult for her to imagine how the affair would come out, she complied with her husband's demands, and invited the friar, informing him that her husband had gone to the country, and would be absent that night. The friar received this message with great joy. At the appointed time he came to the house, and was conducted in by Donna Caterina's maid, not, however, to her lady, but to the master and his trusty varlet, who quietly strangled him. No sooner was the deed done than the lord began somewhat to rue it, and, in order to rid himself of the body, had it conveyed to the convent on his servant's back, and thrust into a privy. It chanced soon after that a young friar, a bitter enemy, by the way, of Maestro Diego, came upon the body, which he discovered by the aid of a small lamp that he carried. Supposing the friar to be alive, he waited for a time, but at length became impatient, and called upon Maestro Diego to make way for him. Receiving no response, and believing himself purposely neglected by the other, he caught up a large stone, and threw it at him. The body fell over limply, and the friar, terrified, bethought himself what he might do. The shameful court paid by Maestro Diego to Roderico's wife then occurring to him, he conveyed the body to Messer Roderico's door, hoping that the murder would be attributed to the jealous husband. The friar's guilty conscience now recommended that he leave the monastery for a time; accordingly he secured permission from the superior to take a mare and fetch certain goods left at Medina, a day's journey distant. Meanwhile Messer Roderico, troubled in mind, sent his servant to listen about the monastery walls. Before the latter had gone far, he found the body outside his door. Master and servant then bound it on the back of a stallion belonging to a neighbor, provided it with a lance, and led the stallion to the front of the monastery, where they tied him to the gate. Just before dawn the friar issued forth on his mare, and was followed by the stallion, which easily snapped the cord with which he had been tied. A wild pursuit through the town then took place, the noise of which called forth the citizens as spectators. The friar, in mortal terror, admitted his guilt, and was turned over to the secular power for punishment. But about this time King Fernando visited Salamanca, to whom Messer Roderico made full confession of what he had done, so that the guiltless friar might not suffer death. Roderico was at once pardoned, and highly commended for his deed.*

Not only in the main incidents employed does Heywood follow Masuccio closely, but many of the details of his story are rendered with considerable fidelity. Thus the lord's momentary inclination to destroy the monastery when he learns of the friar's baseness; the friar's perfuming of himself in preparation for his meeting with the lady, so that there might be nothing about him to suggest the friar; the setting up of the dead friar in the privy; the lord's request that his servant listen about the walls of the monastery—these and other details of treatment reappear in Heywood's version. In several instances the very phraseology reads almost like a translation. On the other hand, Heywood does depart at times from his model, though the reason for the departure is usually apparent. The most striking differences between his plot and Masuccio's narrative are found (1) in the relationship of the lord to the monastery, (2) in the character of the lady, and (3) in the proposal made by the conscience-stricken friar in order to obtain the use of the mare. According to Masuccio, the monastery is not far from Roderico's house; Heywood separates the two buildings by only a brick wall, and has the monastery founded by Roderico. Probably Heywood's object is to cause the friar's deed to appear still baser by making the friar guilty also of the sin of ingratitude, so that his death at the Duke's hands may seem more clearly justified. The Lady of Averne is represented from the first as more noble in character than Donna Caterina. She is annoyed instead of pleased by the friar's letter, informs her lord of the situation at once instead of allowing the friar to court her for a considerable time, and finally is deeply concerned at the thought that her husband may kill the friar, much as she despises him. Heywood has simply trans-

* Masuccio di Salerno, "Novellino," Novel the First, pp. 14-26.

formed a typical Italian lady of the fifteenth century *novella* into
an English lady of his own day. Heywood's change in connection with the friar's application for the use of the mare is doubt-
less made in the interests of plausibility. A friar might reason-
ably propose to the baker before morning that he would bring
flour from the mill for him, but he would scarcely waken his
superior before dawn to suggest a two or three-days' journey.
Besides making these changes, Heywood added two scenes. The
first, which introduces the underplot, gives us a glimpse of the
deep-seated hatred harbored by Friar Richard and Friar John
for each other. The other concludes the underplot: in it the Lady
of Averne is represented as bringing a pardon for her husband's
life, which she has begged from the king. These additions, like
the changes just described, distinctly improve the plot.

No one, after a study of the evidence, can question the fact that
Heywood employed Masuccio's novel, or at least a translation
of it. There is one extant French translation that might have
found its way into Heywood's hands. It appears in Antoine de
Saint-Denis's "Les Comptes du Monde Adventureux,"* first
printed in 1555. Professor Koeppel says of it: "The Frenchman
has followed the Italian closely; the action is identical; only the
French version is throughout somewhat terser in expression."
He then prints the following parallel passages from all three
works:

Il Cavaliere che onorato ed ani-moso era molto fu di tanta fiera ira acceso, che poco si tenne che in quella ora non andasse a porre a ferro e fuoco il Convento e tutti i Frati (p. 117)—	L. AVERNE. . . . this religious place, Once vowed to sanctity, I'l vndermyne And in one instant blowe the structure vpp With all th' vn-hallowed covent (3.1.81)—

Saint-Denis says merely: non sans extreme colere (p. 127);

* Reprinted by Felix Frank, 1878, Compte 23.

lui molto bene perfumatosi, che non desse del fratino (p. 118)—

F. JHON. . . . this capp perfumed of purpose, lest I should smell fryar (3.3.57)—

Saint-Denis: s'estant preparé & accoustré de senteurs & bon vin (p.128);

Ebbe per fermo averlo ucciso lui nel modo detto, e dolente a morte, dubitando che per loro inimicizie di botto sarebbe sospettato in lui (p. 120)—

F. RICH. . . . I have doon a fearefull murder, which our former Inveterate hate will be a thousand testats That I for that insidiated his lyfe (4.2.40)—

With Saint-Denis this ground for anxiety over the supposed murder is lacking; he says merely: [il] estima soudain l'auoir tué, dont fut ce frere si dolent qu'il fondoit tout en larmes (p. 129).*

The conclusion readily drawn from this comparison is that the Italian rather than the French version was in Heywood's hands.

. In addition to giving us the dramatic version of Masuccio's story in "The Captives," Heywood has included a brief account of the same incidents in his encyclopædic "Γυναικεῖον" or "Nine Books of Various History Concerning Women," with the title "The Faire Ladie of Norwich."† As "The Captives" was not licensed till September of the same year, 1624, in which the "Γυναικεῖον" appeared, "The Faire Ladie of Norwich" almost certainly represents the older version. It is written in an extremely pithy style, occupying altogether but three folio pages. It lacks, however, only two important details found in the version of "The Captives": the maid does not appear, and the lord is forgiven at the end without the intercession of his wife. In view of Heywood's different aim in each version, the phraseology is naturally quite different, though a few passages exhibit a rather striking verbal similarity.

No one can study Heywood's use of his sources without having

*Archiv für das Studium der Neueren Sprachen und Litteraturen 97. 328.
†Book V, pp. 253-256.

his admiration excited by the masterly manner in which the dramatist knew how to shape old tales to his own purposes. On the success of his undertaking in the case of "The Captives," Professor Aronstein writes: "The drama exhibits the artist, so far as technic goes, at the height of his art. The two plots, so different in character, Plautus' tale of remarkable loss and recovery and the medieval farce of monks and knights, are with great adroitness united into a thrilling, vivid action."*

Editor's Note.

In the text here given, the spelling of the MS. has been retained, but punctuation and capitalization, both largely lacking, have been supplied according to modern usage.

A few other changes have been made, as follows. The arbitrary or careless separating of words into syllables and occasional joining of two distinct words have been disregarded. Words stricken through and obviously not intended to form a part of the text have been omitted, or, where they appear to exhibit in an interesting way the action of the author's mind in the process of composition, have been reproduced in the foot-notes; but all passages stricken through or marked for omission the reason for whose elimination is not clear have been reproduced as a part of the text and indicated in the foot-notes. Stage directions in a different and evidently later hand (see page 11) have been retained only when they clarify the action. All stage directions have been italicized, and the names of speakers preceding their speeches have been set in small capitals. *Actus* 1 *s*, *Scena* 1 *a*, etc. have been printed *Actus Primus*, *Scena Secunda*, etc.

The difficulty of accurately reproducing the spelling of a crab-

* *Anglia* 37.256.

bed hand has been accentuated by the fact that our copy seems to have been hastily written, with about as many imperfectly formed letters as one finds in the penmanship of ordinary correspondence to-day. The letters *a, e,* and *f* have given me most trouble. The letter *a* is often formed so that *av* looks like *iv* (with *i* undotted), *ay* like *y*. It is often difficult to determine whether we should read *e* or *ee,* and whether a twist at the end of a word is intended for final *e* or a mere flourish. The letter *f* is formed in three different ways, but the *f* most commonly used resembles *ff* (perhaps it is an adaptation of the earlier capital letter). Though I have examined many manuscripts of the period, I have found but one other showing the regular use of what seems to be *ff* for *f,* an indenture between Sir Walter Raleigh and John Fitzjames, 1593, in the possession of the University of California library. As our MS. apparently does not distinguish between the single and the double letter, I have doubled *f* only where modern usage demands it.

For the convenience of the reader I have taken two other liberties with the spelling. I have discarded the long *s* (*ſ*), and I have substituted *j* for *i* where the consonant sound is to be represented (as *j* does not occur in the MS., such a change involves no loss except one of picturesqueness).

In accordance with the practice of the time, certain abbreviations are used. *With, which, nowe,* and *knowe* are almost invariably written *wth, wch, nwe,* and *knwe;* the syllables *per, pir, pre,* and *pri,* and the word *your* are frequently written *p^r* and *y^r;* the stroke below *p* to signify *per* and the stroke over a vowel to signify *m* or *n* are also used. The unabbreviated form has been printed in all these cases.

All words and letters (aside from those just accounted for) that have been inserted in the text have been bracketed. They may be divided into four groups†: (1) letters and words that appear to have been carelessly omitted; in a few cases the omission of a letter may have been intentional, and its insertion must be justified on the ground that the word is thereby made more intelligible to the reader; (2) letters and words apparently torn or cut away from the MS.; (3) letters and words obliterated or almost obliterated from the MS.; in many cases these have been supplied from the Bullen edition, and may be conjectural readings of Mr. Jeayes or Mr. Bullen; (4) letters designed to complete what was probably thought of as an abbreviation.

† Below are lists of all words in whole or in part bracketed (except added stage directions) arranged according to the groups described above. An asterisk means that the word or letter is also bracketed in the Bullen text.

(1) Marr[y] 1.1.68; dam[n]able 1.1.128; dun[g]cart 1.1.159; ag[e]nt 1.1. 197; posse[ss]ion 1.1.239; no[m]ber 1.2.8; brother[s] 1.3.3; fort[u]nate 1.3.84; dam[n]able 1.3.95; vnparrel[lel]'d 1.3.102; mo[u]nt 1.3.118; mis-[c]heifes 1.3.134; vnfreq[u]ented 2.1.64; [Godf.]*2.2.116; make[s] 2.2.156; [Denis.] 3.1.96; ho[r]ses 3.1.121; dam[n]ation 3.2.166, 3.3.66; leng[t]hen 3.3.113; mo[u]nt 3.3.128; pu[n]ctually 4.1.338; handkerch[er] 4.1.376; on[e] 4.1.436; r[u]mors 4.2.48; mo[u]nted 4.2.137, 4.2.145; pay[n]es* 4.2.162; fort[u]nate 4.2.168; infort[u]nate 5.1.16; leng[t]he 5.1.58; [him] 5.1.74; sy[n]ce 5.1.79; fort[u]ne 5.3.78; mo[u]nted 5.3.169, 5.3.311; marcha[n]t 5.3.189; unfort[u]nate 5.3.255; sati[s]faction 5.3.334.

(2) lyv[es] 1. 1. 33; seminar[y] 1. 1. 86; hey[re] 1. 3.36; harbo[r] 2. 3. 95; barbo[r] 2. 3. 97; slee[ve] 3. 1. 3; [this] 3.1. 15; praye[rs] 3. 2. 116; bo[w] 3.2. 124; [me]* 3. 2. 129; crack[t]* 3. 2. 135; hows[es] 4. 1. 36; migh[t] 4. 1.83; howshou[ld] 4. 1. 213; y[ou] 4. 1. 216; vente[r on the] 4. 1. 216; Marcell[is]* 4. 1. 221.

(3) Wi[thin] 1. 1. 56; shamb[les] 1. 1. 117; [them] 1. 1. 118; whormaster[s] 1. 1. 226; he[althe] 1. 2. 57; supp[er] 1. 3. 56; [in] 1. 3. 56; [Yet] 1. 3 . 123; s[oule]* 2. 1. 16; [in] 2. 1. 201; [with] 2. 2. 162; [then] 3. 3. 25; [Lett's remove itt] 3. 3. 88; b[e kept] 5. 3. 108.

(4) Ex[eu]nt 1. 1. 243, 1.2.193, 2.1.193; fish[ermen] 2. 2. 54; Clow[n] 2. 2. 60; l[ord] 5. 3. 270.

My emendations, very few in number, are recorded in the foot-notes, as are all material differences between the Bullen text (hereafter designated as *B.*) and mine. Such stage directions as have been added are followed as well as preceded by a bracket.

[The Captives; or, The Lost Recovered.

Dramatis Personæ.*

The Duke of Averne;

John Ashburne, an English merchant;

Thomas Ashburne, his brother;

Raphael, a merchant;

Treadway, his friend;

Mildew, a procurer;

Sarleboys, his guest and friend;

Friar Richard;

Friar John;

An Abbot;

Dennis, servant to the Duke;

Godfrey,
A Fisherman (Gripus), } servants to Ashburne;

A Factor to Thomas Ashburne;

A Clown, servant to Raphael;

A Baker;

The Lady of Averne;

Palestra, } maidens in the pos-
Scribonia } session of Mildew;

Isabel, wife to Ashburne;

Millicent, maid to the Lady of Averne;

Friars, citizens, attendants, a sheriff and officers.

SCENE: *Marseilles; a village on the shore near the city.*]

*No list of *dramatis personæ* appears in the Bullen edition.

ACTUS PRIMUS

SCENA PRIMA

Enter MR. RAPHAEL, *a yonge marchaunt*, MR. TREADWAY, *his companion and frend.*

RAPHAEL. You talke to one that's deaf; I am resolv'd.
TREADWAY. I knowe you are not of that stupid sence
But you will lyst to reason.
RAPHAEL. All's but vayne.
TREADW. You saye shee's fayre.
RAPHAEL. And there-fore to bee lov'd.
TREADWAY. No consequent, for . . . who so fond   5
To trust to collar. Are not the bewtyous lyllyes,
The garden's pryde and glorye of the feilds,
Thoughe to the eye fayre and delectable,
Yet ranke in smell? The stayneles swanne
With all the ocean's water canott wash   10
The blacknes from her feete; 'tis borne with her.
Oft painted vessayles bringe in poyson'd cates,
And the blackest serpents weare the goldenst skales;
And woman, made man's helper at the fyrst,
Dothe oft proove his destroyer.
RAPHAEL. Saye perhapps   15

frend, etc.] *MS.*
5-27 for . . . frend.] *Marked for omission in MS.*
5 for . . . fond] *Om. B.*

31

Som frend of yours miscarried in his choyse;
Will you condeme all women for that one?
Bycause wee reade one Lais was vnchast,
Are all Corinthian ladyes cortesans?
Shall I, bycause my neighbour's howse was burnt,   20
Condeme the necessary vse of fyer?
One surfetts, and shall I refuse to eate?
That marchant man by ship-wrack lost his goodds;
Shall I, bycause hee perisht in the sea,
Abjure the gainfull trade of merchandyse,   25
Despoyle my shipps, and vnbecom the deepes
Of theire fayre sayles and tackles?

TREADE. Not so, frend.
Allthoughe her person may perhapps content,
Consider but the place.

RAPHAEL. I knowe it badd,
Nay woorst of ills.

TREADWAY. A howse of prostitution   30
And common brothellrie.

RAPHAEL. Which coold not stand
But that her vertue guards it and protects it
From blastinges and heaven's thunder. There shee lyv[es]
Lyke to a ritche and pretious jewell lost,
Fownd shyninge on a doonge-hill, yet the gemme   35
No waye disparadg'd of his former woorthe
Nor bated of his glory; out of this fyer
Of lust and black temptation she is return'd
Lyke gold repur'd and tryde.

TREADWAY. Of what byrthe is shee?

RAPHAEL. Vnknowne to mee or any; shee protests,   40
Naye, to her self. What neede I question that?

33 thunder] thunders *B.*   36 waye] wyse *B.*

Sure sutche sweete feature, goodnes, modesty,
Such gentlenes, such vertue canott bee
Deryv'd from base and obscure parentadge.

TREADWAY. What's then your end and purpose?

RAPHAEL. To redeeme her 45
Out of this gayle of sinne and leprosye,
This mart of all diseases, where shee lyves
Still vnder the comande and tyrany
Of a most base hee-bawde; about which busines
Wee have allready traffict.

TREADWAY. Well, if so, 50
And to dispose her elcewhere to her goodd,
Provided still that vertue be your ayme,
I canott but commende your charity,
And to my power I'l seeke to further it.

RAPHAEL. You so intyre mee to you. Within theire! 55

Enter the CLOWNE.

CLOWNE. Wi[thin] theire is nowe without heare. Your wor-
shipp's pleasure?

RAPHAEL. Hye to the next key and inquire for one cal'd
Seignior Mildewe, and resolve him from mee that I have kept
apointment; the somm's redy and present to be tender'd. 60

CLOWNE. Who? the Neapolitan seignor? the man-makarel
and marchant of madens-fleshe that deales altogether in flawed
ware and crackt comodityes? the bawdy broker, I meanes,
where a man for his dollers may have choyse of diseases, and
som tymes the pox too, if hee will leeve beehind him a goodd 65
pawne for it?

RAPHAEL. Howe thou drumm'st.

42 feature] features *B.*
61 Neapolitan] *Frenshe* monster, *Neapolitan B.* (*See note.*)

CLOWNE. Marr[y], qothe hee. So I may happen to bringe it awaye in my nose. Well, I smell som bawdy busines or other in hand. They call this place Marcellis Roade, the cheif haven towne in France, but hee keepes a road in his owne howse wherein have ridd and bin ridd more leakinge vessayles, more panderly pinks, pimps, and punkes, more rotten bottoms ballanst, more fly-boates laden and vnladen every morninge and evenning tyde then weare able to fill the huge greate baye of Portingall. Is this all, syr?

RAPHAEL. Yes, all, and heare's the some.

CLOWNE. A small somme of that is woorthe all the busines that I am sent about, for the all in all on't is I am afrayde that all will proove woorthe nothinge.   [*Exit.*]

TREADWAY. And yet mee thinkes, ere fully you conclude, You should a little stagger.

RAPHAEL. Speake! Wherein?

TREADWAY. For many reasons. I'l alleadge some fewe. Who knowes but this your fayre and seeminge saynt, Thoughe dispos'd well and in her owne condition Of promisinge goodnes, yet livinge in the seminar[y] Of all libidinous actions, spectars, sights, Even in the open market where sinne's sould, Where lust and all vncleanes are commerst As freely as comodityes are vended Amongst the noblest marchants,—who I saye So confident that dare presume a virgin Of such a soft and maiden temprature, Dayly and howerly still sollicited By gallants of all nations, all degrees, Allmost all ages, even from vpright youth

76 Is] *Scored through in MS.*   80 [*Exit.*]] *Om. B.*
81 fully] folly *B.*   82 Speake] Should *B.*

To th' stoopinge and decrepitt—

RAPHAEL. Heare mee nowe.

TREADWAY. Too woords, and I have doonne: the place considered,

The basenes of the persone vnder whome

Shee lyves opprest, a slave of sordid lyfe,　　　　100

Condition'd with the devill, temptinge still,

Sometymes by fayre means, then againe by force,

To prostitute her for his servyle gayne;

And next the dissolute crewe with which shee's hows'd

Ech night, ech daye, persuadinge boathe with toonge　　105

And lewde example; all these circomstances

Duly considered, I shoold dowbt at least,

If not presume, the woorst.

RAPHAEL. Oh you have pleas'd mee,

And, in proposinge all these difficultyes,

Giuen of her graces ample testimony.　　　　110

Shee is that miracle, that only one

That cann doo these; wear't comon in the sex,

'Twold not appeare to mee so admirable;

It is for these I love her.

TREADWAY. Y'are resolv'd,

And I'l not staye your purpose.　　　　115

Enter the CLOWNE, *with* MILDEWE *and* SARLEBOYS,
his guest and frende.

CLOWNE. I have brought this fleshe-fly, whome as soone as
the butchers' wyves sawe comminge throwghe the shamb[les],
they all of [them] stood with theire flapps in theire hands like
fannes. I demandinge the reason, itt was answer'd mee againe itt

102 force] foul *B.* (*See note.*)　　　103 gayne] gaynes *B.*
114 Y'] You *B.*

was to keepe away his infectious breath least it should fill theire 120
meate with fly-blowes.

    RAPHAEL. Well mett, good Mr. Mildewe.

    MILDEWE. My returne
Of your salutes I cast belowe your feete.

    RAPHAEL. Syr, I am yours to treade on. You will then
Stand to your former bargen?

    MILDEWE. I weare elce   125
Not woorthy to bee stil'd what I am tearm'd,
A trewe venereall broaker.

    CLOWNE. That's in Italian
A dam[n]able hee bawde.

    MILDEWE. Y'have such a bargen
Marcellis, nor all France, shall yeild the lyke.
'Tis such a deynty peece of purity,   130
Such a coy thinge, that hee vnto whose lott
She shall hereafter fall may boast him self
To bee a happy husband. For our trade,
Shee's out at that: neather promises, rewards,
Example, or intreaty, fayre, fowle meanes,   135
Gaine present, or the hope of future goodd,
Can force from her a presens; then much lesse
A frendly prostitution.

    RAPHAEL. Hear'st thou this?

    TREADWAY. Yes, and comende it in her, if that toonge,
Even from his fyrst of speakinge train'd to lyes,   140
Can nowe at lengthe speake truth.

    CLOWNE. Ay, there's the dowbt.

    SARLAB. This too yeares I have quested to his howse,

131-133 that . . . husband.] *Scored through in MS.*
139-141 *Marked for omission in MS.*   140 lyes] lye *B.*
142 SARLAB.] Mildewe. *MS.*

And knowe all this most certeine.

RAPHAEL. Witnes too.

MILDEWE. I doo protest shee spoyles my family,
And rather growne a hyndrance to my trade　　145
Then benefitt; so that, if not to losse,
I wishe that I were clerly ridd of her,
For shee hathe gott a trick to scorne my whores;
And such as of themselves are impudent,
When shee but coms in presens, shee makes blushe,　　150
As if asham'd of what they late had doon,
Or are about to doo.

CLOWNE. Well sayde, ould sinner.

RAPHAEL. See, heere's the sum, 3 hondred crownes.

MILDEW. O, th' somme!

RAPHAEL. All currant and full weight.

MILDEW. I'l fetch my doughter
That hathe no lightnes in her, currant too　　155
As any lass i' th' cittye.

RAPHAEL. Mildewe, staye.

CLOWNE. Staye, oh thou father of fornication and marchant of
nothinge but miseryes and myscheife; wheele about, thou
dun[g]cart of diseases; sayle this way, thoue gally-foyst of galls
and garbadge! Dost not heare my mayster? Staye!　　160

MILDEWE. Why, did his woorshippe call?

CLOWNE. Didst thou not heare him call, and mee cry out vpon thee?

MILDEWE. His pleasure, then?

RAPHAEL. I have bethought mee better nowe to keepe　　165
This busines secrett, least it chanc to arryve
To th' eares of some of my most noble frends;

148 scorne] . . . *B.*　　　　158 miseryes] mesteryes *B.*

And not to make it publicke and this honest
Purpose of myne by that meanes misreated,
Heare lett her stay till night, bycause I am loath   170
In th' eye of daye to move her through the streetes.

MILDEWE. Good, syr.

RAPHAEL. Nowe in the villadge by, that fronts the sea
Som half league off, where stands the monastery,
I have bespoake a place to sojorne her.   175
There I this eveninge do intend a feast
Where only wee and som fewe private frends
Have purpost to bee jhoviall. To that place
I prithee, with what pryvacy thou canst,
Conduct her, and so add vnto our guests.   180

MILDEWE. The place I knowe, the tyme is perfect with mee,
And, for the feast you saye you have prepar'd,
I shall provyde a stomacke.

RAPHAEL. Her caskett, and such other necessaryes
Included in our bargen, bringe along,   185
Or lett her mayde doo't for thee.

MILDEW. I'l not bate her
A ruff or ragge; no pinne that's vsefull too her
Will I keepe backe.

RAPHAEL. To this you are witnes, frend.

TREADWAY. I am, syr.

MILDEW. So's my guest.

CLOWNE. And lookes as if with me   190
Hee only could wryte witlesse.

RAPHAEL. Supper tyme
You will remember, Mildewe.

MILDEWE. Possible

176 do intend] *A correction in MS. for* have beespoke.
190, 191 CLOWNE . . . witlesse.] *Marked for omission in MS.*

I shoold forgett to eate of others' cost?
It never was my custom.

   CLOWNE. Choake you for't.

   RAPHAEL. Com, frend; mee thinks I have doone a deede
    this day   195
Crownes all my better actions, for I have raised
An innocent from the hands of an infidell ag[e]nt.

   CLOWNE. Farewell, rott; farewell, murreine; adiewe.

   MILDEWE. Farewell till soone.

      [*Exeunt* RAPHAEL, TREADWAY, *and* CLOWNE.]

   SARLAB. And do you meane to keepe your promisse then,   200
And doo as you have sayde?

   MILDEWE. Why not, I prithee?
What elce canst thou advyse mee?

   SARLAB. Are not wee
Boathe of a rotten consciens, men debosht,
Secluded from the company of such
As eather are or elce would stryve to bee   205
Reputed honest? Wherefore then should wee
Keepe tutch with any that professe themselfes
Not to bee of our ranke?

   MILDEWE. Proceede, good frend;
Thou hast putt project in my brayne allredy,
Small tyme woold better fashion.

   SARLAB. What if I   210
Laye such a plotte that you shall gayne these crownes,
These full three hundryd, to your proper vse,
And of these peevishe harletryes at home
Make a much greater market?

   MILDEWE. Marry, syre,
That were a tale woorth listeninge.

   199 MILDEWE . . . soone.] *In MS. a continuation of Clowne's speech.*

SARLAB. These crowns   21
Are all your owne, in your possession;
So are the maydes. I knowe you ritche beesydes
In coyne and jewells; heere you lyve despys'd,
And what's this clime to vs of more esteme
Then any forreine region? Whores and bawdes   22
May lyve in every corner of the woorld—
Wee knowe 'tis full of sinners. This, this day
Lett's hyre a barke; wee dwell vpon the haven,
And instantly 'tis doon. Shipp all your goodds
With these shee-chatteyles; putt this night to sea.   22
England they saye is full of whormaster[s].
There will be vent for such comodityes;
There strompett them where they (you saye) weare born;
Elce you in Spayne maye sell them to the stewes,
Venyce, or any place of Italy: 23
They are everywhere good chaffer. If not these,
What saye you to Morocho, Fesse, Algeires?
Faith, these are wares in all parts vendible,
No matter thoughe to Turke and infidell,
So itt bringe gayne and profitt.
    MILDEWE. Lett me hugg thee   23
For this, deare frend; heareafter I will style thee
My better genius; thou hast monied mee in this,
Nay landed me, made me thy brayne's executor,
And putt mee in a lardge posse[ss]ion.
Go hyre a barke.
    SARLAB. I shall.
    MILDEW. And instantly.   24
    SARLAB. I shall.

222 This . . . day] *A correction in MS. for* instantly.
226 whormaster[s]] *A correction in MS. for* merchandyse.

MILDEWE. Ere night wee'l putt into a sea
No lardger then our full stretcht consciences.
Lett mee once more imbrace thee.   [*Ex*[*eu*]*nt.*

ACTUS PRIMUS

SCENA SECUNDA

Enter an ABBOT, *with his covent of fryars, amongst them*
FRYAR JHON *and* FRYAR RITCHARD.

ABBATT. As I have heare priority of place,
Boathe by our patron's favour and your voyce,
So giue mee leave to arbitrate amongst you.

F. JHON. Without respect of person wee acknowledge you
Our prince and cheife.

F. RICHARD. And to your fatherly   5
And grave advyse humbly submitt our selves.

ABBOTT. Knowe then in this small covent, which consysts
Only of 12 in no[m]ber—fryars, I meane—
And vs the abbat, I have fownde amongst you
Many and grosse abuses; yet for the present   10
I will insist on fewe. Quarrells, debates,
Whisperinge, supplantinges, private callumnyes,
These ought not bee in such a brotherhoodd.
Of these Fryar Jhon and thou, Fryar Richard, are
Accus'd to bee most guilty, ever jarringe   15
And opposite to peace.

F. JHON. The fawlt's in him.

1 *Marginal stage directions in another hand:* Chairs. Jack, Gibson.

F. RICH. As in all other thinges, so even in this
Hee still is apt to wronge mee.

F. JHON. Hee that fyrst giues th' occation fyrst complaines;
It ever was his fashion.

F. RICH. Never myne;   20
I appeale to the whole covent.

ABBOT. Mallyce rooted,
I finde, is woondrous hard to bee supprest.
But knowe, where consell and advise preveyle not,
The fayrest meanes that I can woork your peace,
I'l take vpon mee my authority;   25
And where I finde in you the least contempt,
I shall severely punishe.

F. JHON. I submitt.

FRY. RICH. I yeild myself to your grave fatherhoodd.

ABBOTT. Consider, sonnes: this cloyster'd place of ours
Is but newe rear'd; the fownder, hee still lyves,   30
A souldier once and eminent in the feild,
And after many battayles nowe retyr'd
In peace to lyve a lyf contemplativ.
Mongst many other charitable deedes,
Vnto religion hee hathe vowed this howse,   35
Next to his owne fayre mantion that adjoynes
And parted only by a slender wall.
Who knowes but that hee, neighboring vs so neare
And havinge doone this vnto pious ends,
May carry over vs and our behaviours   40
An austere ey of censure?

F. JHON. Fitt, therefore,
Wee should bee in our actions cautelous.

FRYAR RICH. And carefull least wee may incurr displeasure
Of such a noble patron.

ABBOT. Well observ'd.
His bewtious lady—
　F. JHON. A sweete soule indeede.　　　　　　　　45
　F. RICHARD. On whom Fryar Jhon casts many a leering ey;
I have observ'd that, too.
　ABBOT. Boath for her outward feature
And for her inward graces, exellent
Beyond compare; shee lykewyse is to vs　　　　50
A woorthy benefactor.
　F. RICH. 'Tis confest.
　F. JHON. Would I might com to bee her confessor;
It is a fayre, sweete lady.
　F. RITCH. Howe the lecher
Hugges at the very name.
　ABBOT. Morninge and eveninge
They dayly com to mattens and to evensonge.　　55
Such and so greate is theire devotion
That, if not cras'd or faylinge in theire [he]althe,
They do not misse vs any hower of prayer;
And therefore it behooves vs all in generall
To sett a carefull watche vpon our deedes,　　60
Least we that are profest religious
Be in the least defectiue.
　F. RITCHARD. Noate Fryare Jhon,
Howe hee makes anticke faces, and in scorne
Of this your reverent counsell.
　F. JHON. I? Alas,
A weakenes from my childhood, I confesse,　　65
I ever had, and canott helpe it nowe,
To have a trobled countenance. I make mouthes?
This, most observed father, but approoves

53, 54 F. RITCH. . . . name.] *Marked for omission in MS.*

My innocens and his envye. Markt you that?
Fryar Richard bent his fyst and threatned mee.   70
I call all these to witnesse.

     F. RITCH. No such thinge!
I have a crampe oft takes mee in this hand,
And makes mee weare clutcht fingers, and that passion
Nowe came vpon mee; but for meanacinge him,
It ever was farr from mee. This but showes   75
His owld, inveterate mallyce, which in charity
I wishe might heare lye buried.——Syrrah, anon
I'l have you by the eares.

     F. JHON. Doo if thou dar'st;
We'll tugge it out by the teeth.

     F. RITCHARD. Meete me i' th' orchard
Just after even song.

     F. JHON. I will make short prayers   80
Bycause I'l keepe appointment.

     ABBOTT. I am playne
And breife with all: eather beetwixt you too
Make frendly reconsilement, and in presence
Of this your brotherhood (for what is fryar
But frater, and that's brother?), or my selfe   85
Out of my power will putt you to a penance
Shall make you in one weeke fyve fasting-dayes.

     F. JHON. Oh terrible!

     ABBOTT. Or, if that will not tame you,
I will complayne to th' fownder of your loosenes,
Your riotts, and disorders, and petition   90
That you, as sowers of seditions heare
And sole disturbers of our comon peace,
Maye bee excluded this society,

     91 seditions heare] seditious hatred [?] *B.*

Banisht by comon barre-law, and shutt out
To publick shame and beggerye.

 F. RICHARD. Horrible!   95
 F. JHON. Fyrst, then, to showe my submisse willingnes
And forwardnes withall, with as much charity
As any new reformed man maye doo,
I with a zeale & hart new reconcil'd
Thus humbly begge his love. (Y' are a rogue, Ritchard.)
 F. RICHARD. To meete his trewe   100
And most vnfeigned affeċtion, heare in face
And viewe of this our holly brotherhoode,
As if in open coort, with this imbrace
I heare confine all hatred. (Jhon, y' are a Jack sauce, I meane
  a sawcye Jacke.)
 F. JHON. The orchard.
 FR. RICHARD. Theare.
 ABBOT. Why, this is as it should bee, and beecomes   105
A trew religious order. Such as are sequestred
And vowed vnto a strickt monasticke lyfe
Ought to putt off these grosse and prophane sines
Most frequent amongst laye-men. Vnity,
Due conformation, and fraternall love;   110
Devotion, hott zeale, and obediens; these
Are vertues that become a cloyster best.
Nowe lett's retyre vnto our oresons
And praye for our good fownders; may they still
Growe to our wishe and thryve to theire owne will.   115
       [*Exeunt all but* FRIAR JHON.]
 F. JHON. More then I woold to have my wishe on thee,
Ritchard, though I have a good stomacke too't,
Ey, and to baste thee sowndly, I woold nowe

 103 imbrace] mi [?] breath *B.*

To have my will on her. 'Tis a sweete creature;
Our patron owld, shee younge; som hope in that.   12¢
Besydes, shee's woondrous kind and affable;
And when we duck or congee, smiles as if
Shee tooke som pleasure in our shaven crownes.
I am the fyrst that every morninge, when
Shee passes through the cloyster to her prayers,   12ξ
Attend her with good morrowe, pray for her health,
For her content and pleasure, such as canott bee
Hop't or expected from her husband's age;
And these my frendly wishes shee returnes
Not only in kind languadge but sweete smiles,   13c
The least of which breede some incoradgement.
I will, if shee persist to proove thus kind,
If not to speake my thoughts, to wryte my mynd.

                                            [*Exit.*]

ACTUS PRIMUS

SCENA TERTIA

Thunder.

Enter, after a greate, tempestuous storme, MR. ASHBURNE,
an English marchant, and his man, GODFREY.

ASHBURNE. Was ever knowne such a tempestuous night
Of thunder, hayle, wynd, lightninge! 'Twas as if
The fower seditious brother[s] thretned warr,
And weare but nowe at battayle.
    GODFREY. The fower winds, you meane; blustringe fellowes 5

119 on] one *B. MS.?*

they are. Preye God all bee well at sea, for I am suer the roofes'
tyles and ridges have payde for it ashoar.

ASHB. The very rafters of the howses bend;
Some breake and are demolisht; barnes blowne downe;
The very chimnyes rattle ore our heads;   10
The strongest buildinges tremble just as, if
Theire is aboue a tempest, so beelowe
There weare a fearefull earth-quake.

GODFREY. All our howses
Are nothinge nowe but windowes, broad bay windowes
So spatious that carts laded may drive throughe   15
And neather brush o'th' topp or eathere syde.
Lights every where, wee shall have lightnes inoughe;
Heare's stupid woork for daubers!

ASHBURNE. We are forſt
All to forsake the villadge and to fly
Vnto the feilds for succor.

GODFREY. Syr, it putt me   20
In minde of the greate King Agathocles,
Who was, as I have heard you oft relate,
Brain'd with a tyle. Why may not meaner men,
Then, feare the fall of brick batts?

Enter RAPHAEL, TREADWAY, *and the* CLOWNE.

TREADWAY. A strange night
And full of terror; yet, thanks heaven, well past.   25

RAPHAEL. Oh, but I feare the greater storms to come,
A gust that will more shake mee.

CLOWNE. More, quothe hee; I can scarce see howe that well can
bee, for I can assure you the garrett that I laye in putt mee in
mind of myne infancy, for I laye all the night longe as if I had 30
bin rockt in a cradle.

16 brush] loush *B.*   30 laye] lye *B.*

RAPH. Oh, frend, I feare this false and perjur'd slave,
That hathe not kept apointment, hath deceiv'd mee
Boathe of my coyne and pretious marchandyse.

CLOWNE. Did you ever looke for better from a Judas of his   35
hey[re]?

RAPH. Which if hee have—

CLOWNE. Why then hee hathe, and the mends is in your owne
hands; that's all that I can saye too't.

RAPHAEL. Hee hathe vndoon mee dubly.

TREADWAY. Hope the best.   40
Perhapps the threatninge weather kept him backe:
Itt was a trobled skye, the soon set blushing,
The rack cam swiftly rushing from the west;
And these presadges of a future storme,
Vnwillinge to trust her tendernes   45
Vnto such feares, might make him fayle his hower;
And yet with purpose what hee slackt last night
Nowe to make goodd this morninge.

RAPHAEL. Oh you tent
My woonds too gently, dally with my dowbts,
And flutter my trewe feares; the even was calme,   50
The skye vntrobled, and the soon went downe
Without disturbanc in a temperate ayer.
No, not the least conjecture coold bee made
Of such a suddeine storme, of which the woorld
Till after midnight was not sensible.   55
His hower was supp[er], and [in] faylinge that—

CLOWNE. Ey, nowe begin I to feare too for thee. Breake his
woord if itt bee to com to dinner or supper! I'l never trust his
bond for the valewe of a threepenny ordinarye after.

35 Judas of his hey[re]] Judas [?] of his he[yre] *B.*   45 to] [for] to *B.*
48 Nowe] Howe *B.*

RAPHAEL. Post you back to the citty; make inquiry　　60
And most strickt search tó find that Mildewe out;
Whome if you meete, fyrst rate his last neclect,
Then hasten his repayer. Heare you shall finde mee
Or in the waye home; for in all this villadge
I will not leave a howse, a place, vnsearcht.　　65
If where hee dwells you misse him, then demande
Att every key what shippinge late went out.
If any vowed love still remane betwixt vs,
Make it appeare nowe in your present care
And expedition.

TREAD. I'l be your Mercury,　　70
Not fayle you in the least.

RAPHAELL. And so beetwixt vs
Increase a frendshipp that was never flawed.

[*Exit* TREADWAY.]

ASHBURNE. This gentleman, itt seemes, hathe in this tempest
Sustein'd som losse, hee appeares so much disturb'd.

CLOWNE. See, syr, heare are some itt may bee beelonge to this　75
villadge; you had best aske of them.

RAPHAEL. And well advys'd. Hayle, father!

GODFREY. No more hayle if you love mee; we had too much
of that last night.

ASHBURNE. Of what sex are you that you call mee so?　　80
I have bine father of a doughter once,
Though not these many yeares blest with her sight,
But of a soone yet never.

RAPHAEL. What you have lost
May you in som most fayer and fort[u]nate hower
Againe find to your comfort.　　85

60 inquiry] inquiries *B.*　　　　　67 key] bey *B. MS.?*
　85 find] *A correction in the MS. for* recover.

ASH. You wishe well.

RAPHAELL. Sawe you nott bowte this villadge late last night,
Or early nowe i' th' morninge, a short fellowe,
Thin-heyr'd, flat-nos'd, sand-beareded, and squint-eyde?

CLOWNE. The mapp of misfortune and very pictur of ill luck.

RAPHA. Grosse wasted, gowty-legg'd.   90

CLOWNE. Whose face is puft vpp lyke a bladder, and whose
belly lyke a toonne.

RAPHAEL. Owld, graye, and hoary.

CLOWNE. And withall cheatinge, cousininge, and crafty; a re-
markeable raskall, a dam[n]able deceaver, and a most substan-   9
tiall sinner.

ASHBURNE. By such I have much suffred in my state,
Opprest allmost to vtmost penury
In my once better fortune; but so late
I sawe not any such.

RAPHAEL. Hee was expected   10
To bee attended by too handsome guirles,
Boathe yonge, boathe fayre, but th' one vnparrel[lel]'d;
Neather of which by computation
Hathe told so hye as twenty.

ASHBUR. If such I chance to meete by accident,   10
I'l send you notyce. Please you leave your name
And place of your aboade.

RAPHAEL. Raphael, I am cal'd,
A marchant in Marcellis, and my lodginge
Is at the Parratt in the markett-place;
There you shall finde mee knowne.

ASHBURNE. And by that name   11
Presume I'l not forgett you.

93-96] *Marked for omission in MS.*

RAPHAELL. For which curtesy,
Fare you well, syr;
You shall oblighe mee to you. If not heare
Wee'le seeke her further; France shall not conteine them
But I will finde theire start-holes.

　ASHBURNE. Good speede with you.　　115

　CLOWNE. If I weare a dogge nowe and coold hunt dry foote, I
could smell them out presently.

　　　　　　　[*Exeunt* RAPHAEL *and* CLOWN.]

　ASH. Come, lett vs mo[u]nt our selfes vpon these rockes,
And, havinge feelinge of our hurts at land,
Lett's see what shyppes have bin distrest at sea,　　120
If any shaken in this storme or wrackt;
And though wee cannot help the miserable,
[Yet] lett them taste our pittye.

　GODFREY. Sir, content; but I hope your fishermen have not
putt to sea this night. If they have, I sweare they have showed 125
them-selves much madder then the tempest.

　ASHBURNE. I hope they have bin more discreate and wyse
Then with the hazard of my boates and netts
To indanger theire owne lyves.

　GODF. See! do you see, syr?

　ASHBUR. What?

　GODF. Why, yonder.

　ASHBURNE. Where?　　130

　GODF. There towards yon shore.

　ASHB. A shipp laboringe for lyfe,
Nowe cast vpon the rocks, nowe splitt, nowe sinkinge,
Nowe dasht to peeces.

　GODFREY. I see all mis[c]heifes do not com by land,
Som's doone vpon the water.

113-117] *Marked for omission in MS.*　114 them] this *MS.*

ASHBURNE. Though theire goods perishe,
Yet in thy mercy, heaven, protect theire lyves.
Som sitt vpon the planks, som on the masts,
Som hange vpon the cables, and som few
Have only gott the cock-boate; others swimme.
Oh that wee shoold beehold theire misery,
And want power to assiste them!

GODFREY. Sure, syr, it was som shipp of passengers,
For see you not too women? Daynty ducks!
Would they coold swime as ducks can. Look how they sprall
And cast theire legges abroad lyke naked frogges!
See how they spread theire armes and stryve for lyfe!
I woold I weare som dolphin or some whayle
That they might sitt astryde vpon my backe
To beare them safe ashore; but I as yet
Coold neare indure still water. See yet still,
Still theire coates beare them vpp, keepe them aloft;
The modest ayer not willinge to discover
That which the bawdy waves shame not beelowe
Rudely to lifte and handle.

ASHBURNE. Blesse them, heaven!
The wind and tyde still beate them towards the shore,
But oh that cursed billowe hathe devyded
And parted them asunder. Yet all's well;
They still beare vpp. If they but scape the next,
There may bee hope of safetye.

GODF. One's driven this way,
The tother that. The men shift for them selves;
Howe shall wee save thes women?

ASHB. No meanes vnlesse we leape downe from the rockes,

144 Look how they sprall] see how they spread *B.*
147-150] *Marked for omission in MS.*

And that's meare desperation. Yet to showe
Our charityes to wretches thus extreame,
Lett's see if wee can find the least discent　　　　　165
And hasten to theire suckor.

　GODFR. By your favour,
I had rather they with brine shoold breake their bellys
Then I my neck with clambringe.　　　　　*[Exeunt.]*

　　　　EXPLICIT ACTUS PR.

　168 [*Exeunt.*] *Om. B.*

ACTUS SECUNDUS

SCENA PRIMA

Storme contynewed. Enter PALESTRA, *all wett, as
newly shipwracke and escapt the fury of the seas.*

PALESTRA. Is this, then, the reward of innocence,
Of goodness, to our selfes, namely chast lyfe,
Pietye to our parents, love to all,
And, aboue all, our Christian zeale towards heaven?
But why shoold wee poore wretches thus contest   5
Against the powers aboue vs when even they
That are the best amongst vs are serv'd badd?
Alas, I never yet wrong'd man or child,
Woman or babe; never supplanted frend
Or sought revendge vpon an enemy.   10
You see yet howe we suffer; howe shall they, then,
That false theire faythes, that are of vncleane lyfe,
And then not only sinne vnto them selves,
But tempt and persuade others? What shall I thinke
Becoms of my base guardien? Though the waves   15
Have spared the guiltles, suer his putrid s[oule]
Canot escape heaven's justyce! Wee poore wretches
Are punisht for his grosse impietyes;
They moov'd heaven's wrathe, who stir'd the wynds & waves,

wett] *well B.*   shipwracke] *shipwreckd B.*
8-32] *Marked for omission in MS.*
18 punisht] *punishe MS.*

55

Stryvinge whose fury shoold destroy vs fyrst.   20
These boathe conspyringe in our ruin, th' one
Beate vs beelowe the billowes whylst the other
Swallowed boathe shippe and goodds, amongst the rest
A budget, or portmantua, which included
All the bawde's wealth. But that weare nothinge to mee   25
Though hee had vowed and sworne to make mee his heyer;
The losse I so lament is a small caskett
Kept by him from my childhood, and packt vp
Amongst his treasure; and that perishinge,
I forfett the longe expectation   30
Ever to knowe my parents, there-fore wishe
With it I had i'th' sea bin buried.

Enter SCRIBONIA.

SCRIBONIA. With perill of oft fallinge and the danger
Of second deathe, havinge new scapt the fyrst,
I have with feare and terror clim'd these rocks,   35
And these too past, I feare to meete a thyrd.
I spy no howse, no harbor, meete no creature
To point mee to som shelter; there-fore heare
Must starve by famine or expire by could.
O' th' sea the whystlinge winds still threaten wracke,   40
And flyinge nowe for refuge to the lande,
Find nought save desolation. Though these three,
Three dreadfull deathes all spare mee, yeat a fowerth,
I can not shoone in my Palestrae's losse,
More deare to mee then all the world besydes,   45
For the best bloodd of myne ranne in her veynes,
This lyfe breathe in her boosom. Oh my Palestra!

24 included] includes *B.*   40 wracke] wreckes *B.*
45] *Scored through in MS.*   46 ranne] runns *B.*

PALESTRA. Numnes and feare, hungar and sollitude,
Besydes my casket my Scribonia's losse—
All these at onc afflict mee.

 SCRIB. Nothinge mee   50
More then Palestra's death. Ha, who's that spake?
Suer 'twas som woman's voyce! If my Palestra,
Only for her sake I coold wishe to live.

 PAL. Then lyve, my deere Scribonia, synce I am only
Spar'd to pertake with thee newe miseryes.   55

 SCRIB. Scarce can I bee perswaded you are shee;
But, bee yt but her shadowe, giue mee leave
For her remembrance to imbrace it thus.

 PALEST. These armes att onc locke all my lyvinge hopes
In my reserv'd Scribonia.

 SCRIBO. Nowe I perceave   60
My comfort is not meare imadginary
But reall and effectiall. Lyve you then?

 PALEST. To triumphe in your safety.

 SCRIB. Possible
That mongst these desert vnfreq [u] ented rocks
Thou can imadgine such a thing can bee   65
As that which you call safety?

 PALESTRA. Yes, Scribonia,
And comfort too; for, see, I spye a villadge,
A maner and a fayre built monastery,
Just att the foott of this descendinge hill.
And where, if not amongst religious men,   70
Shoold wee find that's call'd charity?

 SCRIB. Thether, then,
Lett vs make hast with all the speede wee can:

60 reserv'd] restored *B.* (*See note.*) 68 built] build *MS.*
72] *Scored through in MS.*

Fyre att the least I hope it will affoord,
Besydes releife and harbor.
　PAL. Can you begge?
　SCRIB. What will not rude necessity compell　　　　75
Distressed folke to doo? Wee'l not doo't basely,
For beinge brought vpp to musick and to sing,
Demandinge in that kind there charity,
And they perceivinge vs much better bred
Then these our present fortunes might deserve,　　　80
May move in them compassions.
　PALEST. Lett's retyre
To the backe gate then, there complane our wants,
And that which others doo with impudence
Lett vs in shame and blushes.
　SCRIB. Som sweete echo
Speake from these walls and answer to our wants,　　　85
And eather lend som comfort to our greifes,
Or send vs hence dispayringe and asham'd.

　　　　　　　　　　　　　　[*They go in.*

　PAL. Oh charity, where art thou fledd,
And nowe how longe hast thou bin dead?
　ANSWER WITHIN. Oh many, many, many hondred yeares.　90
　SCRIB. In villadge, borrough, towne, or citty
Remaines there yet no grace, no pitty?
　ANS. Not in sighes, not in want, not in teares.
　PAL. Cold comfort in this answer; but proceede.
Aboue we see a threatninge sky.　　　　　　　　　95
　ANSWE. Beelowe the winds and gusts blowe hye,
And all, all to fright hence this same juell.
　SCRIB. The lightninges blast, the thunders crack,
The billowes menace nought save wracke.

　73 it will affoord] it [is?] well assured *B.*

ANSW. & yet man is then these much more crewell.   100
  PAL. Vnless my judgment quite miscarry,
Shee may lyve in som monastery.
  ANSW. 'Tis a place too that was fyrst assign'd her.
  SCRIB. If not amongst religious men,
Yett where, where shall we seeke her then?   105
  ANSW. Yet even there, there, you scarce, scarce can find her.
  PALEST. If chastity and innocens tryde
Have boathe escaped wind and tyde—
  ANS. Yet, oh, why should the land, land these cherish?
  SCRIB. Of whome even billowes have a care,   110
Whome seas preserve, whome tempests spare—
  ANS. Yet these, these amongst men may perishe.
  PALESTRA. Vncharitable echo! From a place
Of pure devotion canst thou answer that?
If not in these religious monestaryes,   115
In what place can wee find could charity?
  SCRIBONIA. Where ere wee meete her, shee is lyke our selfes,
Bare, without harbor, weake and comfortles.
                Enter FRYER JHON.
  F. JHON. What singinge beggers weare those at the gate
That would so early rowse our charity,   120
Before it was half styrringe or awake?
                Ent. FRYER RICHARD.
I thinke I answer'd them in such a key
As I beeleeve scarce pleas'd them.
  F. RICHARD. What sweete musick
Was that at the back gate hath cal'd mee vpp
Somwhat beefore my hower?

  105 seeke] *A correction in MS. for* find.
  110 billowes] *A correction in MS. for* tempests.
  122 key] way *B.*

F. JHON. Morrow, Fryar Richard;   125
Howe did you lyke our last night's buffetinge?
Whylst all the rest of our fràternity
In feare of that greate tempest weare att prayers,
We too pickt out that tyme of least suspition,
And in the orchard hand to hand weare att it.   130
    F. RICHARD. 'Tis trew for blooddy noses; and, Fryar Jhon,
As you lyke that which is allredy past,
So chalendge mee hereafter. But whence came
Those sweete and delicate voyces?
    FRYAR JOHN. I bare part
In theire sadd quire, though none of these yet know't.   135
But peace: our father abbat.

                Enter the ABBOT, *with other fryars.*

    ABBOT. Morrow, soonns;   ·
An early blessinge on you, if as the larke
Ryson betymes still to salute the soon,
So your devotion pluckes you from your bedds
Before your hower vnto your orisons.   140
Did you not heare a musicall complaynt
Of women that in sadd and mournefull tones
Bewayl'd theire late desasters, harshly answer'd
By a churlish echo?
    F. JHON. Some such thinge wee heard.
    F. RICHARD. The noates still persist [?] with mee.
    PALESTRA. There appeares   145
In his grave lookes boathe zeale and charity;
Lett's to his sight boldly expose our selfes.
Hayle, reverent father!
    ABBOTT. What are you, poore soules,
Thus wett and wether-bitt?

SCRIBONIA. Ere you demand
Further from vs, lett's tast your Christian charity.   150
Som fyare, som harboure, least ere our sadd tale
Be fully tould wee perishe.
    ABBOT. Why, whence came you?
    PALESTRA. From sea; our shipp last night in the great storme
Cast on these rocks and splitt; this the fyrst place
Expos'd vnto our eyes to begge releif.   155
But, oh, I faynt.
    ABBOT. Some faggotts instantly;
Hott brothes, hott water for them, and warme cloathes.
Whome the high powers miraculously preserve,
Whome even the merciles waves have borne ashore,
Shall wee see sinke a land? Even wee our selfes   160
That lyve and eate by others' charity,
To others shall not wee bee charitable?
All succor, all supply that can bee giuen,
They from our hands shall tast.
    F. JHON. Shall wee remove them
Into the cloyster?
    F. RICHARD. 'Tis agaynst our oath   165
On any, though the great'st, extremity
To addmitt weomen thether.
    ABBOTT. That I knowe;
& yet in som out-office see them chear'd,
Want nothinge that the cloyster can affourd.
Theire bewtyes, though my eye be bleynd att them,   170
Deserve no lesse; I looke on theire distresse,
And that I pitty. Ech one lend a hand
To take off from theire present misery

    156, 157 Some . . . clothes.] *Scored through in MS.*
    160 see] soe *B.*   168 &] *Om. B.*

And ease theire tender shoulders; when they are cheer'd
And better comforted, I'l finde occatione　　　　175
To enquire further from them.

PALESTRA. Heaven be as kind
To you as you to vs!

ABBOTT. Feare not, fayre damselles;
This place, though not within the monastery,
Yet stands within the cloyster's priviledge,
And shal bee vnto you a sanctuary.　　　　180

SCRIBONIA. No other wee expect it.

ABBOTT. Guide them in:　　　　　　　[*Bell rung.*
Bewty and youthe to pitty 'tis no sinne.

　　　　　　　[*Exeunt* PALESTRA *and* SCRIBONIA.]
　The bell ringes to mattens. Enter the LORD DE AVERNE *and*
　　　his LADY, DENNIS *and others.*

F. JHON. Harke, the bell ringes to mattens.

F. RICH. See withall
Our noble patroon with his lovely lady
Prepar'd for theire devotion. Nowe, Fryar Jhon,　　　185
Your leatcherous ey is conninge.

F. JHON. I knowe my place.

ABBOTT. Way for our noble fownder!

L. AVERNE. Morrowe, father;
So to the rest of all the brotherhoodd.

　　　　　　[*The quire and musick; the fryars make*
　　　　　　　　a lane with ducks and obeysance.

VOYCES. Te tuosque semper, oh semper beamus,
Et salvos vos venisse, O venisse gaudeamus.　　　190

F. JHON. Good day to our fayre fowndresse!

LADY. Mercy, Fryar Jhon;

182 [*Exeunt* PALESTRA *and* SCRIBONIA.]] *Om. B.*
185 Prepar'd] Prepare *B.*

Aboue the rest you are still dutifull,
For which wee kindly thanke you.

　　　　　　　　　　[*Ex[eu]nt; manet* JOHN.

　F. JHON. Kindly thanke you!
Nay, smil'd with-all! Allthough that I have more
Then a monthe's mind to these yonge harletryes,　　　195
Yet heare's the grownd on which I fyrst must build
And rayse my fortunes many storyes hye.
Nay, I perhapps, ere they can drye there smocks,
Will putt th' affayre in motion, whyle these are
Att solleme mattens. I'l take pen and wryte,　　　200
And sett my mind downe [in] so quaint a strayne
Shall make her laughe and tickle, whylst I laugh
And tickle with the thought on't, still presuminge
These lookes, these smyles, these favours, this sweete languag
Coold never breathe butt have theire byrthe from love.　　　205
But how to ha'tt delivered? There's the dowbt.
Tush, I have plott for that too; hee, no question,
That sett mee on to compasse this my will
Maye, when the up-shoote comes, assist mee still.　　　[*Exit.*]

ACTUS SECUNDUS

SCENA SECUNDA

　　　　　　　　　　　　[*Tempest; thunder.*
　　　　Enter 2 FISHERMEN.

I FISHER. The trobled sea is yet scarce navigable
　Synce the last tempest; yet wee that only lyv
By our owne sweett and laboure, nor cann eate

　197 rayse] ryse *B.*　　　storyes] steepes *B.* (*See note.*)

Before wee fetch our foode out of the sea,
Must venter thoughe with danger, or bee suer
With empty stomakes go vnsupt to bedd.
  2 FISHER. And so it often happens.
  1 FISHER. See the cordadge
Be stronge and tight, the netts with all theire stringes,
Plometts, and corks, well plact; for hookes and bates—
This daye wee shall have little vse of them.   10
The wind's still hye; beare but a gentle sayle,
And hazard not the channell. Keepe alonge
Close by the shoare; the rocks will shelter vs,
And may perhapps afford vs lobsters, praunes,
Shrimps, crabbes, and such lyke shell fishe. Heare we may 15
Hunt the sea vrchin, and with safety too;
There's many holde him for a dayntye fishe;
Hee sells well in the markett. That poore men
Are forct too, for a slender competens,
A little to prolonge a wretched lyfe!   20
  2 FISHER. Com then, lett vs weighe anchor and aboord;
The soonne is vpp allredy.

Enter the CLOWNE.

  CLOWNE. If ever menn weare madd, then suer my mayster is
not well in his witts, and all about this wenshe; here's such send-
inge and seekinge, hurringe and postinge, and all to no purpose. 25
I have nowe some thyrty errands to deliver, and knowe not to
whome nor where, what nor to which place fyrst; hee's gone on
to the citty and sent mee back to the villadge, whither his frend
travel'd one waye, hee another, and I a thyrd contrary from them
boathe; he cannott beleeve his inquiry to be well doone, but hee 30
must send mee to doo't over againe. I have askt all I mett and

---

demanded of all I have seen, only, for ought I can perceive, all
to no purpose. I can vnderstand of no such people. But what are
these? Though they have slipt vs, no creature shall slippe mee.
These should bee fishermen. Good morrowe, you sea theeves. 35

  1 FISHER. You call vs theeves that may proove honester
Then many goe for trewe men on the shore.

  CLOW. Sawe you not passe this waye an ould, bald fellowe,
hutch-shoulder'd, crooked nos'd, beetle brow'd, with a visadge
lowringe and a looke skoolinge; one that heaven hates and ev- 40
ery good man abhorrs; a cheatinge raskall and an vgly slave,
—did none such passe you?

  1 FISHER. If such a one as you describe you inquire for,
Mee thinks, my frend, thou hast mistooke thy way.
Thou shouldst have sought him at the gallowes rather;   45
There such are soonest fownd.

  CLOWNE. Berlady, worst answered of a playne fellowe; but that
you may knowe him the better, hee had too handsom, swete,
smugge-fac't lasses in his companye.

  2 FISHER. And for such creatures y'had best search the stewes 50
I' th' citty; this our villadge yeilds none such.
This fellowe doth butt flowte vs; lett's aboord.

  1 FISHER. Inquire for vs of wenshes? Tush, wee fishe
For no such perewinkles. Fare well, flesh monger.

              [*Ex.* FISH[ERMEN.]

  CLOWNE. No woonder these fellowes pretend to bee witty; 55
for vnderstandinge, so manye have lost there witts (as . . . they

32-35 seen . . . These] seene. But what are theese? these *B.*
32-34 only . . . mee] *Printed by B. as foot-note.*   33 I can] but *B.*
34 Though . . . mee] *Scored through in MS.*
34 these? Though they have] these things that have *B.*
34 creature] countrie *B.*   38 waye] [way] *B.*
42 none] note *B.*   48 swete smugge-fac't] streete-singing-faćt *B.*
51 I' th'] O' th' *B.*

have fisht for it and in som drawenett or other have caught it.
But where might these lost shrewes bee? I suspeɛ̃ this pestiferous Je vous prie hathe putt some slovenly tricke or other to
cheate my mayster boathe of his ware and mony.   6

      Enter SCRIBONIA, *with an empty pale, to yᵉ* CLOW[N].

    SCRIBONIA. Thus beeinge chered with warmth and change
      of clothes,
With all such comforts as the cloyster yeilds,
I am dyreɛ̃ed to a neighbour's by
For water to refreshe and wash our selves.
And this shoold bee the howse.

    CLOWNE. What! not Scribonia,   6
One of the flock that's missinge?

    SCRIBO. Oh sweete Jayms,
Where is your noble maister?

    CLOWNE. Nay, sweete rogue,
Where is his bewteous mystresse?

    SCRIB. Heare within.

    CLOWNE. In this place joyninge to the monastary?
And Mildewe too?

    SCRIB. Rott on that villeine! No.   7

    CLOWNE. Hee promist to bringe you too alonge and meete with
my master and som others of his frends att supper.

    SCRIB. Can such men, ever false vnto theire God,
Keepe faythe with men at any tyme?

    CLOWNE. But staye, staye; there's one riddle I canott ex- 7
pound. Howe com thou so suddenly to lepp out of a howse of
roguery into a howse of religion, from a stewes to a cloyster, from
beastliness to blessednes, and from a sacriligious place to a sanctuary?

    SCRIB. Such was the grace heaven lent vs, who from perill,   8

    80 lent] sent *B.*

Danger of lyfe, the extream'st of all extreames,
Hathe brought vs to the happy patronadge
Of this most reverent abbott.

 CLOWNE. What dangers? what extreames?

 SCRIB. From the sea's fury, drowninge; for last night   85
Our shipp was splitt, wee cast vpon these rocks.

 CLOWNE. Sayd in a jest, indeede! Shipp-wrack by land! I perceive you tooke the woodden waggen for a shipp, the violent
rayne for the sea, and bycause some one of the wheeles broake
and you cast into some water plash, you thought the shipp had 90
splitt and you had bin in danger of drowninge.

 SCRIB. Are you then ignorant howe, late in the even,
With purpose to make better sale of vs
And to defraude thy maister, hee shipt vs
With all the gold and jewells that hee had,   95
All which save wee are perisht?

 CLOWNE. But that caterpiller, that ould catamiting canker
worme, what's become of him?

 SCRIB. Dead I hope, with drinkinge of salt-water.

 CLOWNE. I would all of his profession had pledged him the 100
same healthe. But howe doth Palestra take this?

 SCRIB. Gladd to bee ridd of such a slavery,
Yet sadly weepinge for her caskett's losse,
That which included ample testimony
Bothe of her name and parents.   105

 CLOWNE. All her ill luck go with it! I'l fyrst in and see her,
bycause I will bee suer 'tis shee. Oh, Mercury, that I had thy
winges tyde to my heeles. Heere will bee simple newes to bringe
to my mayster when hee hears she hathe bin shipp-wracke! I'l
make him beleeve I went a fishinge for her to sea, and eather 110

88 shipp] shipp and *MS. B.* (and *scored through in MS.*).
106-108 I'l . . . heeles.] *Scored through in MS.*

drewe her ashore in my netts, or, batinge my hooke, strooke her
and drewe her vpp by the gills with myne angle. Make you hast,
for I'l stay till you com back.   [*Exit.*]

    SCRIB. But this delaye had allmost putt mee from
What I was sent about; yes, this the place.   [*Knocks.* 11

Enter GODFR.

    [GODF.] Whoe's that that offers violens to these gates
That never yet offended? What want you?
    SCRIB. That which the earth
Dothe forbidd none, but freely yeilds to all,
A little fayre springe water.
    GODF.—One of those guirles   120
Belyke this morninge shippwrackt and nowe scapt,
A dainty peece of mayde's fleshe. Such sweete bitts
Are not heare often swallowed, and my mouth
Waters at this fine morsell.
    SCRIB. Water, frend;
'Tis that I crave, for heaven sake.   125
    GODF. We have none
Of guift, vnless you by't.
    SCRIBON. Will you sell that
The earthe affoords you gratis, and sett pryse
Of what a foe woold yeild an enemy?
    GODF. Not, prety lasse, so thou'lt afford mee that,
Freely and without bargen, which not only   130
One frend will to another but oft tymes
A stranger to a stranger.
    SCRIB. What's that, prithee?
    GODFRY. Only a kisse, sweete wensh.
    SCRIB. Ye are too familiar;

115 this] this is *B.*   119 but] and *B.*
125 heaven] heaven's *B.*

I'l by none at that pryse. Or fill my pale,
Or I'l returne back empty.
　　GODF. Well, for once　　　　　　　　　　　135
I will not greatly stand out, yet in hope
That what att our fyrst meetinge you'l not grant
You'l not denye at partinge; reatch thy pale.
　　SCRIBO. Quick, as you love mee.
　　GODF. As you love mee! right;
Who ever lov'd that lov'd not att fyrst sight?　　140
The poet's exellent sayinge.　　　　[*Exit to draw water.*]
　　SCRIB. What shall I saye or howe shall I excuse
This my longe staye? But nowe I cast myne eyes
Back on the roughe yet vnappeased seas;
I quake to thinke vpon our dangers past.　　　145
But see the fearefull object of a death
More menacinge and affrightfull, a sea monster
Cast from the deepes to swallowe vs ashore!
Malevolent fate and black desaster still
Pursues vs to all places, but of all　　　　　150
　　　　　　Ent. MYLDEW *&* SARLABOYES *to her.*
This, this the greatest, and to this one compar'd
All that are past but trifles. Oh that grand master
Of mechall lusts, that bulke of brothelree,
That stillary of all infectious sinnes,
Hathe scapt the wrack, and with his fellowe guest　　155
And partner in corruption make[s] this waye,
And with no tarde pace. Where shall I hyde mee?
Whether shall I fly? I'l to Palestra back,
And with this sadd relation kill her quite
That's scarce recovered! Rather you hy powers,　　160
Then to prolonge our greifes, shorten our howers.　[*Exeunt.*]

　　158 I'l] *Om. B.*　　　　　　161 [*Exeunt*]] [*Exit*] *B.*

Enter GODFREY, [*with*] *water.*

GODF. Where is my daynty damosella? where?
Mee thought the water mett mee the half way
And lept vpp full three stepps to meete my pale.
This 'tis whenas a man goes willingly   16
About his busines. Howe fresh a kisse will tast
From her whyte lipps! And every part besydes
From head to toe have bin so lately duckt
And rincht in the salt water. Where's my sweete?
Not heare? no where? why, hoe, my whytinge mopp   17
Late scapt from feedinge haddocks! ha, what, gone?
Nay then, go thou too that shee sent mee for,
To him that next shall find thee! Yet not so;
This learned pale instructs mee by these letters
That it beelonges vnto this monastery.   17
And if it shoqld be lost by my default,
I may bee chardg'd with theft or sacrilidge.
No, I'l deliver it to the owners suer,
And this the place.   *[Exit.]*

ACTUS SECUNDUS
SCENA TERTIA

Enter the bawde MILDEWE *and* SARLABOYSE.

MILDEW. Hee that woold stooddy to bee miserable,
Lett him forsake the land and putt to sea.
What widging, that hathe any voyce att all,

Enter GODFREY [*with*] *water.] Scored through in MS. Om. B.*
162-179] *Marked for omission in MS.*
179 And . . . place.] *A substitution in MS. for the following lines, which have
been scored through:*
And not deteine, for feare't bee to my cost,
Though boath my kisse and all my paynes be lost.
179 [*Exit.*]] *Om. B.* ACTUS SECUNDUS SCENA TERTIA] *Om. B.*

Would trust his safety to a rotten planke
That hathe on earthe sownd foottinge!
   SARLAB. None but madmen.   5
   MILDEWE. Why, thou of none, thrifty and well advised;
Stryv'st thou to make mee such? Where's now the gayne
And profitt promist, the ritche marchandyse
Of lust and whooringe, the greate vsury
Gott by the sale of wantons? These cursed wretches,   10
With all the wealthe and treasure that I had,
All perisht in one bottom, and all, all,
Throughe thy malitious counsell.
   SARLABOYES. Curse thy selfe.
The trusty barke, ore laden with thy sinnes,
Baudryes, grosse lyes, thy thefts and perjuryes,   15
Beesydes the burdene of thy ill gott goodds,
Not able to indure so greate a weight,
Was forct to sinke beneathe them.
   MILDEW. Had not thy greater fraught bin shipt with myne,
She had never bin oversett.
   SARLAB. I rather thinke   20
Had wee, when fyrst the shippe began to dance,
Rold thee with thy curst ladinge overboard,
Wee had sayl'd light and tight.
   MILDEWE. Out, dogge!
   SARLAB. Out, devill!
   MILDEWE. By thee I am made nothinge. Oh my guirles,

10 wretches] jewelryes *B.*   15 thefts] theft *B.*
19-23 MILDEW . . . tight.] *Marked for omission in MS; printed by B. as footnote.*
20 She] We *B.*   21 wee] . . . *B.*
22 Rold thee with thy] . . . thrown all the *B.*
23 sayl'd] still *B.*

You sweete and never faylinge marchandyse,
Comodityes in all coasts, woorthy coyne,
Christiane or heathen, by whome in distresses
I coold have rays'd a fortune! More vndoon
That I should loose you thus!

  SARLAB. I knowe hee had rather
See half a hondred of them burnt a land
Then one destroyde by water. But, oh Neptune,
I feare I have supt so much of thy salt brothe
'Twill bringe mee to a feavour.

  MILDEW. Oh my Palestra
And fayre Scribonia, weare but you too safe,
Yet som hope weare reserv'd me.

  SARLAB. I praye, Mildewe,
When you so early to the bottom dyv'd,
For whome weare you a fishinge?

  MILDEW. Marry, for maydes;
Woold I knewe howe to catche them. But my gutts,
Howe they are swel'd with sea brine!

  SARLAB. 'Tis good phisicke
To cure thee of the mangy.

  MILDEWE. Wretched man,
That have no more left of a magazin
Then these wett cloathes vpon mee, nay the woorst
Of all I had and purposely putt on
Only to lyv a shipp-board.

  SALRAB. Once to-day
Thou wert in wealthe aboue mee; nowe the seas have
Left vs an equall portion.

  MILDEW. In all the woorld

37 maydes] maydens *B.*

I vowe I am not woorthe a lighted faggott
Or a poore pan of charcoale.

    SARLAB. Justly punisht,
Thou that hast all thy lyfe tyme dealt in fyrewoorkes,
Stoves and hott bathes to sweet in, nowe to have   50
Thy teethe to chatter in thy head for cowld
Nimbler then virginall jacks.

    MILDEW. Th' art a sweet guest.

    SARLAB. Too good for such an host; better to have bin
Lodg'd in som spittle; or, if possible,
To bee imprisoned in som surgeon's box   55
That smells of salves and plasters.

    MILDEWE. Nowe what sharke
Or wyde-mouth'd whale shall swallowe vpp my budgett,
May it at th' instant choake him!

    SARLAB. Cursedly 'twas gott,
And nowe thy curse goes with it.

    MILDEW. But those guirles!
Nought so much greives mee as to part with them   60
Before they lost theire maiden-heads. Had they lyv'd
Till I had seen them women, and o 'th' trade,
My cost and care bestowed to bringe them vpp
I should have thought well spent, which nowe with them
Is meerely cast away.   65

          Enter GODFREY.

    SARLAB. Peace now your pratinge, and heare another . . . .

    GODFRY. The pale religious, which was the pledge
Of a kisse lascivious, I have giuen backe,

51 chatter] falter *B.*
52-56 MILDEW . . . plasters.] *Marked for omission in MS.*
63 cost] tast *B.*   66 . . .] spirit *B.*
67-80] *Marked for omission in MS.*

Ey, and to boote the water. But within
There's such a coyle betwixt the 2 yonge guirles,　　70
Such quakinge, shakinge, quiveringe, shiveringe,
Such cryinge, and such talke of flyinge, then of hyding,
And that there's no abydinge. One cryes out and calls;
The other's redy to breake downe the walls;
Then weepinge, they whisper together,　　75
And saye they woold roone if they knew whether,
And are indeede putt to such strange affrights
That I was afrayde they weare hunted with sprights,
And therfore rann and left them; lass, poore guirles,
They are in piteous feare.　　80

　　MILDEWE. Hee talkt of guirles; why may not these be they,
Escapt as wee? Stay, yonge man, good frend, staye.

　　GODF. Too ould drown'd ratts—I'l have som sport with them,
And though I pitty those, I'l play with these.

　　MILDEW. What gurles weare those thou spakest of?

　　SARLAB. Tell vs fyrst　　85
Where wee might finde som comfort.

　　GODFREY. Lett vs, oh lett vs, be advys'd,
And livinge still to all men,
So though we bee but midle siz'd,
We shal bee held no small men.　　90

　　MILDEW. Concerning these fayre damosels, speake of that.

　　SARLAB. Which nowe concernes vs most, where may wee meete
With warmth, with foode, and shelter?

　　GODF. Oh thou that dost demand of mee
Som fyre, som meate, & harbo[r],　　95
I see thou lately hast bin washt;
Hath Neptune bin thy barbo[r]?

　　78 sprights] springht *MS.*　　　　　79 rann] cam *B.*
　　93 shelter] *A correction in MS. for* comfort.

SARLAB. This fellowe mearely flowtes our misery,
And laughs att our distresses.

MILDEW. But, kind frende,
Concerninge these yonge women, are they fayre? 100

GODFREY. Fayre, fresh, and cleane they boathe appeare,
And not lyke gypsies vmber'd.

MILDEW. How many?

GODFREY. Just as thou and I
When wee are once but numbred.

MILDEW. Oh, Sarlebois, there's comfort in these woords; 105
They have allredy warm'd my hart within.
Why may not these bee they?

SARLAB. Bee they or not,
I had rather see one caudell downe my throate,
To wash downe this salt-water, then bee mayster
Of all the wenshes lyvinge.

MILDEW. Oh where, where, 110
Where might I see too such?

GODF. Thou that goest sydewayes lyke a crabb,
Gap'st on mee lyke an oyster,
Followe thy flat nose & smell them there,
In th' out part of this cloyster. 115

MILDEWE. Oh maye this peece of earth prove happy to mee
As hath the sea bin fatall.

SARLAB. I'l followe and coold wish
Boath cloyster and whole villadge weare a fyre
Only to dry my clothes by.

GODFREY. Marry, hange you, 120
You that so late scaped drowninge, for I take you
For too pestiferous raskalls.   [*Exeunt.*

EXPLICIT ACTUS SECUNDUS.

101 fresh] flesh *B*.

ACTUS TERTIUS

SCENA PRIMA

Enter the LADY DE AVERNE, *with a letter in her hand, readinge,*
and with her MAYDE.

LADY. And howe came you by this?
    MAYDE. Followinge you to th' chappell
    And, I protest, not thinkinge anythinge,
Fryar Jhon o' th' suddeine pluckt mee by the slee[ve],
And whisper'd in myne eare to giue that to you,
But privatly, bycause it was a thinge   5
Only toweard your person.
    LADY. 'Twas well doonne.
But prithee do no more so; for this tyme
Tak't for a warninge.
    MAYDE. Madam, I am skool'd.
    LADY. Doo so, or ever loose mee. Heere's sweet stuffe!
Can this bee in a vowed monastick lyfe,   10
Or to bee fownd in churchmen—nothinge but love,
And all syr-reverens like. 'Tis a question
Whether to smyle or vex, to laughe or storme,
Bycause in this I finde the cause of boathe.
What might [this] sawcy fellowe spy in mee   15
To incorradge such a boldnes? Yes, this letter

9 Heere's . . . stuffe !] *Scored through in MS.*
11, 12 nothinge . . . like.] *Scored through in MS.; Om. B.*

77

Instructs mee what; hee seythe my affability
And modest smiles, still gracinge his salutes,
Moov'd him to wryte. Oh what a chary care then
Had womene neede have boathe of lipps and eyes   20
When every fayre woord's censur'd liberty,
And every kind looke meere licensiousnes!
I have bin heatherto so greate a stranger
To these vnvs'd temptations that in trothe
I knowe not howe to take this. Sylly fryar!   25
Madnes or folly, one of these 't must bee.
If th' one I pitty, att the other laughe,
And so no more reguard it.

    MAYDE. Madam, if ought bee in that letter ill,
Mee thinks 'tis good that you can tak't so well.   30

    LADY. Peace, you; a braineles, weake, besotted fellowe!
But lett mee better recollect my self.
Madnes nor folly, and add lust to them,
Durst not in fury, heate, or ignorans,
Have tempted my vnquestion'd chastity   35
Without a fowrthe abetter, jealosy.
The more I ponder that, I more suspect
By that my lord should have a hand in this,
&, knowinge there's such differens in our yeares,
To proove my faythe might putt this triall on mee.   40
Elce howe durst such a poore penurious fryar
Oppose such an vnheard of impudens
Gaynst my incensed fury and revendge?
My best is there-fore, as I am inocent,
To stooddy myne owne safety, showe this letter,   45
Which onc my charity woold have conceal'd,

29 MAYDE] Madam *MS.*   30 that] [that] *B.*
39] *Scored through in MS.*   46 onc] one [?] *B.*

And rather giue him vpp a sacrifice
To my lord's just incensement then indanger
Myne owne vnblemisht truth and loyalty
By incurringe his displeasure; heare hee coms.   50

Enter the LORD DE AVERNE *with som*
followers; his man DENIS.

L. AVERN. Nowe, lady, readinge?

LADY. Yes, a letter, sir.

L. AVERNE. Imparts it any newes?

LADY. Yes, syr, strange newes,
And scarce to bee beleaved.

L. AVERNE. Forreigne?

LADY. Domestick;
'Tis howshould busines all.

L. AVERNE. May I impart it?

LADY. Oh, syr, in any case,   55
As one it most concernes; but I intreate you,
Reade it with patiens; the simplicity
Of him that writte it will afford you mirthe,
Or elce his mallice, spleene.—Nowe by his temper
And change of countenance I shall easily find   60
Whose hand was cheife in this.

L. AVERNE. All leave the place.

DENIS. We shall, syr.   [*Exeunt all but the* LORD *and*
L. AVERNE. Possible   LADY OF AVERNE.]
That this shoold bee in man, nay in man vowed
Vnto a strickt, abstemious chastity!
From my owne creature and from one I feede,   65

51 Nowe] Howe *B.*

53 Domestick] Nay, domestick *B.* (Nay, *which destroys the meter, has been scored*
through in MS.)

62 [*Exeunt all but the* LORD *and* LADY OF AVERNE.]] *Om. B.*

Nay from a place built in my holliest vowes,
Establisht in my purpose, in my lyfe
Maintayn'd from my revenue, after death
Firm'd and assur'd to all posterityes—
That that shoold breede such vipers! 70
    LADY. Patiens, syr; the fellowe suer is madd.
    L. AVERNE. I can be madd as hee too, and I will.
Thus to abuse my goodnes! In a deede
Som woold hold meritorious, att the least
Intended for an act of piety, 75
To suffer in my zeale! Nay to bee mockt
In my devotion by these empty drones
That feede vpon the honey of my hyve!
To invert my good intendements, turne this nest
I built for prayer vnto a bedd of sinnes! 80
Which thus I'l punish; this religious place,
Once vowed to sanctity, I'l vndermyne
And in one instant blowe the structure vpp
With all th' vnhallowed covent.
    LADY. Y' are in extreames;
Where one offends, shall for his heighnous fact 85
So many suffer? There's no justyce in't.
    L. AVERNE. Som justyce I will showe them heare on earthe
Before they finde it multiplyed in heaven.
    LADY. For my sake, syr, do not for one man's error
Destroy a woorke of perpetuity, 90
By which your name shall lyve. One man offends;
Lett the delinquent suffer.
    L. AVERNE. So't shal bee,
And thou hast well advys'd. Som pen and inke theire!

    79 *Marginal note:* Ink: paper ready. *MS. B.*
    84 Y' are in] Praye, no *B.*   87 will] would *B.*

LADY. What purpose you?

L. AVERNE. That's soly to my selfe,

And in my fyxt thoughts stands irreproovable.   95

   Enter DENNIS *with pen, inke & paper.*

[DENIS.] Syr, heare's pen, inke, and paper.

L. AVERNE. To his letter

My self will give an answer.   [*Wrytes.*

 DENIS. Suer all's not well that on the suddeine thus

My lord is so distempered.

  LADY. I have, I feare,

Styr'd such a heate that nought save bloodd will quensh, 100

But wishe my teares might doo't; hee's full of storme,

And that in him will not bee easily calm'd.

His rage and troble boath pronounce him guiltles

Of this attempt, which makes mee rather doubt

Hee may proove too seveare in his revendge,   105

Which I with all indevour will prevent.

Yet to the most censorious I appeale,

What coold I lesse have doone to save myne honor

From suffringe beneathe skandall?

  L. AVERNE. See, heare's all;

'Tis short and sweete. Wryte this in your owne hand 110

Without exchange of the least sillable.

Insert in copinge no suspitious dash,

Or doubtfull comma; then subscribe your name,

Seal 't then with your owne signet, and dispatche it

As I will have dyrected; doo't, I charge you,   115

Without the least demurre or fallacy.

By dooinge this you shall prevent distrust

Or future breach beetwixt vs; you shall further

96 [DENIS.]] *Om. B.*   97 an] him *B.*

113 Or] No *B.*

Expresse a just obediens.

   LADY. Syr, I shall;

What ere your conceal'd purpose bee, I shall.   12

   L. AVERNE. Provyde mee ho[r]ses; I will ryde.

   DENIS. When, syr?

   L. AVERNE. Instantly, after dinner, and gee't out

I am not to returne till three dayes hence;

So spreade it throughe the howse.

   DENIS. What followers, syr,

Meane you to take alonge?

   L. AVERN. Thy self, no more,   12

For 'tis a private busines; and withall

Provyde mee,—harke, thyne eare.

   DENIS. A stronge one, syrr.

   L. AVERNE. One that will howld; withall giue private order

At night the guarden gate may bee left ope,

By which wee may returne vnknowne to any.   13

What I intend lyes heare.

   DENIS. All wee servants

Are bownd to doo, but not examine what;

That's out of our comission.

   L. AVERNE. 'Twixt vs too

I shall resolve thee further.

   DENIS. I am gone, syr.   [*Exit.*]

   L. AVERN. Nowe, sweete lady, have you doon?   13

   LADY. As you comanded.

   L. AVERNE. It wants nothinge nowe

But seale and superscription; I'l see't doone.

And marke mee nowe; at evensonge, passinge through

The cloyster to the chappell, when the fryar

Amongst the rest bowes with his woonted duckes,   14

   129 gate] gates *B.*   ope] open *B.*   134 [*Exit.*]] *Om. B.*

Add rather then deminish from your smiles
And wonted favours. Lett this shee post then
Conveigh this letter to the fryer's close fist,
Who no dowbt gapes for answer.

    LADY. All shall bee
As you instructe; but punishe, syr, with pitty;   145
Putt him to payne or shame, but deathe, alas,
Is too seveare example.

    L. AVERNE. Tush, wyfe; feare not. Think'st thou I'le quale
a churchman?   [*Exeunt.*

ACTUS TERTIUS

SCENA SECUNDA

Enter, after a great noyse within, the CLOWNE, *meetinge
with* ASHBURNE *and* GODFREY.

CLOWNE. If this villadge be inhabited with men as this place
within is with monsters; if with men that have eyes and
can distinguishe bewty, or that have harts and therfore sauer
of pitty; if you bee fathers and knowe what belonges to children,
or Christianes and therfor what is ment by charity; if hus-   5
bandmen and have hope of your harvest, or marchants of your
trade's increase; if fishermen that would thryve by your labours,
or any of all these that would be knowne by your honesty —

    ASHBURNE. Many of those thou namest have place in vs,
The great'st part, if not all.   10

    CLOWNE. Then lend your helpinge hands to succor, releive,

147 example] *Om. B.*
10 The] *Om. B.*

defend, deliver, save, secure, patronadge, abett, and mayntayn—

ASHBURNE. Whome, what?

CLOWNE. Bewty, vertue, purity, syncerity, softnes, sweetenes, inocens, and chastity.

ASHB. Gainst what? gainst whome?

CLOWNE. Oppression, frawde, rudenes, reprosh, sin, shame, debate, distrust, theft, rapine, contempt of religion, and breach of sanᵭtury, against a magazine of misdemeanors and a whole monopoly of mischeif.

GODFREY. I knowe the busines, syr, if in that place
These are the too distressed wracks at sea
We sawe this morninge floatinge; sweeter guirles
I never yet sett ey on, and opprest
By too ill lookinge raskells that to warme them
Wisht all the towne a bonefyre—

ASHBURNE. Miscreant slaves!
For one yonge damsell's sake I once cal'd daughter,
And in the absens of there greater frends,
I'l stand beetwixt them and these injuryes.

CLOWNE. These are they after whome I have bin seekinge, and my mayster was inquiringe. If you will but secure them heare in the villadge whilst I carry woord to my mayster in the citty, you shall doo mee a curtesye and him a most noble offyce.

ASHBURNE. It was no more then promisse, and I shoold
Fayle in my goodnes not to see that doonne.
Post to thy mayster, bid him meete vs heare;
Meane tyme my menn shall rayse the villadgers,
Boathe in the reskewe of these inocent maydes
And in defens of holly priviledge.

CLOWNE. I fly lyke the winds.

12 secure] serve *B*.   18 distrust] discourse *B*.

GODF. And I'l go call the pesants
To rayse another tempest.

[*Exeunt* CLOWN *and* GODFREY.]

ASHBURNE. Hasten boathe,
And till ayde com I'l laye myne eare and listen
To heare what further coyle is kept within—
All's silent on the suddeine.　　　　　　　　　　　45

[*Musick.*

[*Song within.*]

[1] Helpe, helpe, oh ayde a wretched mayde,
　　or els we are vndoon then.
[2] And have I caught, and have I caught you?
　　In vayne it is to roonne then.
[1] Som reskewe then from gods or men　　　　　50
　　redeeme vs from these crosses!
[2] 'Tis all in vayne, since nowe I gaine
　　part of my former losses.
[1] Oh heaven, defend! What, yet no end
　　of these our strange desasters?　　　　　　　55
[2] No favour's knowne; no pittye's showen
　　to them that fly there maysters.
[1] Why to defame, reproch, and shame,
　　poore innocents thus dragge yee?
[2] With your offens there's no dispence;　　　　60
　　away then! Wherefore lagge yee?

A tumult within and suddein noyse. Enter att one doore GODFREY,
　　with coontry fellowes for there reskewe, at the other
　　MILDEWE, SARLABOYS, PALESTRA, SCRIBONIA.

PALEST. Where, in what place, shall wee beestowe our selfes
From this injust man's fury?

50 then] when *MS.*

SCRIB. If compel'd
And dragg'd from sanctuary by prophane hands,
Where shall wee flye to safety?

ASHBURNE. Wheither, if   6
Not vnto vs? We often see the gods
Giue and bequeathe there justyce vnto men,
Which we as faythefully will see perform'd.

ALL. Downe with these saucy companiones!

GODFRAY. Downe with these sacraligious silsepaereales, these   7
vnsanctified Sarlaboyses that woold make a very seralia of the
sanctuary, and are meare renegadoes to all religion!

MILDEW. Stay, hold, are you bandetty, rovers, theives,
And wayte you heare to robb and pilladge vs
The sea so late hathe ryfled? These are myne,   7
My chattells and my goodds, nor can you cease them
As wracks; I appeale vnto the admirall.

ASHB. His power I in his absens will supply,
And cease yee all as forfett; these as goodds,
You as superfluous ladinge, till that coort   8
Shall comprimise betwixt vs.

MILDEW. I' th' meane tyme
Lett mee possesse myne owne; these are my slaves,
My vtensills, my mooveables, and bought
With myne owne private coyne.

SARLAB. To which I am witnes.

MILDEW. And by the heyre I'l dragge them as myne owne,   8
Wear't from the holly alter.

PALEST. Succor!

SCRIB. Helpe!

ASHBUR. Are they not Christians?

MILDEW. Yes.

ASHBUR. What nation?

MILDEW. Englishe.

ASHBUR. In myne owne coontry borne, and shall not I
Stand as theire champion then? I tell thee, pesant,
England's no broode for slaves.

PALEST. Oh, syr, to you   90
Wee fly as to a father.

ASHBURNE. And I'l guard you
As weare you myne owne children.

MILDEWE. Gainst there lord,
Owner, and mayster?

ASHBURNE. None is lordd with vs
But such as are freeborne; our Christian lawes
Do not allowe such to bee bought or sould,   95
For any bawde or pandar to hyre such
To comon prostitution. Heere they stand;
Tutch but a garment, nay a heyre of theres
With thy least finger, thy bald head I'l sinke
Beelowe thy gowty feete.

MILDEW. I am opprest;   100
Is theire no lawe in France?

ASHBUR. Yes, syr, to punish
These chastitye's seducers.

MILDEW. Giue mee fyar;
I will not leave of all this monastery,
Of you or these, of what's combustible,
Naye of my self, one moiety vnconsumed.   105

GODFREY. His frend beefore him wisht the towne a fyre;
Nowe hee would burne the cloyster: too arch-pillers!

ASHBURNE. And lyke such
Our purpose is to vse them. Dare not, miscreant,

100 feete] foote *B.*   105 one moiety] *A correction in MS. for* dispeyring.

Onc to giue these a name whome thou calst thyne,   110
No not a beck or nod; if thou but styr
To doo vnto this howse of sanctity
Damadge or outrage, I will laye thee prostrate
Beneathe these staves and halberts.

MILDEW. Is this lawe?

GODFREY. Yes, Stafford's lawe.

ASHBURNE. Naye, feare not, prety guirles;   115
The fryars them selfs, weare they not at theire praye[rs],
Wold have doon more then this in just defens
Of theire immunitys; but in theire absens
I stand for them, nor shall you part from hence
Or dare to squetche till they themselves be judges   120
Of injurye doone to this sacred place,
Or such as I have sent for make appearance
To clayme what thou vnjustly calst thyne owne.

GODFREY. Nay, thou shalt find wee have too stringes to our
bo[w].

ASHBURNE. If hee but styrr, then stryke.

MILDEW. This Stafford law,   125
Which I till nowe heard never nam'd in France,
Is for the present a more fearefull coort
Then chancery or starr-chamber. I want motion;
You have made [me] a statue, a meere imadge.

GODFREY. Styrr and thou diest. Wee'le maule you.   130

MILDEW. If heare I can have none, lett me depart
To looke elcewhere for justyce.

SARLAB. Keepe him prisoner,

110 onc] But *B.* name] menace *B.*
120 squetche] sqeelche *B.*   judges] judge *B.*
124 shalt find] shall stand *B.*   132 looke] seake *B.*
130-139] *Marked for omission in MS.*

And sett mee free to find some advocate
To pleade in his just cause.

GODFRE. Neather styrr
In payne of too Frensh crownes, and they so crack[t]　　135
Never more to passe for currant.

ASHBURNE. That presume.

MILDEW. Misery of miseryes! I am bownd hand and foote,
And yet boath legges and armes at liberty.

GODF. Yes, by the lawe cal'd Stafford.

Enter MR. RAPHAEL, MR. TREADWAY,
and the CLOWNE.

RAPHAEL. Durst then the slave vse my Palestra thus,　　140
And dragge her by the heyre from sanctuary?

CLOWNE. Most trew, syr.

RAPHAEL. Why did'st not kill him?

CLOWNE. If I had had but a swoard, I had doon't; but I sought
the villadge through, and coold find neare a cutter.　　145

RAPHAEL. Weare there no skattered stones lye in the streete
To have beate his braynes out?

CLOWNE. Not a stone to throwe att a dogg.

RAPHAEL. Had'st thou not heeles?

CLOWNE. Yes, to have kickt him lyke a dogge, but I reserv'd　150
them to roon the more nimbly about your busines.

PALESTRA. I nowe spye a newe sanctuary, his armes,
In which I may pursue security.
My Raphael!

RAPHAEL. My Palestra, are you safe?
Beefore I giue due thankes to this good man,　　155
Which tyme shall paye in all pluralityes,
Oh shewe mee but that monster of mankind
And shame of men on whome to bee revendg'd!

154 are you] art thou *B*.

MILDEW. The storme at sea was not more terrible
Then this the land nowe threatens; againe vndoon,   160
Over and over wretched!
    CLOWNE. See the limbe
Of his ould syre, the devill.
    RAPHAEL. Perjur'd slave!
Perfidious, but that I abhore to take
The hangman's office from him, this should open
A doore by which thy black soule should fly out   165
Vnto assured dam[n]ation.
    TREADWAY. Bee more patient;
Proceede with him after a legall course,
And bee not swayde by fury.
    RAPHAEL. Well advys'd:
What can thy falce toonge pleade in thy excuse,
Thou volume of all vyces?
    MILDEWE. Why, what not?   170
    RAPHAEL. Is thy hart sear'd, thy browe made impudent,
And all thy malefactions arm'd with lyes
Against just testates and apparant truthes?
When I had payde full ransom for this pryze,
Why did'st thou beare her hence?
    MILDEWE. I did not doo't,—   175
These bee my witnes; have I borne her hence
When I have brought her to thee?
    RAPHAEL. Thy bawde's rethorick
Shall not excuse thee thus. Frends, guarde him safe.
    CLOWNE. Wee will see his foole's coate guarded, ey and reguard-
ed too from slipping out of our fingers.   180
    GODFREY. Wee'l finde amongst vs more then to make him fow-

172 arm'd] crownd *B.*   181-184] *Marked for omission in MS.*
181 to make] . . . *B.*

er elbowes. Elbowe him off all sydes, gentlemen. Itt shall appeare beefore hee parts with vs that hee hathe showed him self
no better then a coxcombe.

   TREADWAY. Beleeve mee nowe, I do not blame my frend   185
To fishe in trobled streames for such a pearle,
Or digge in black mowld for so ritch a myne;
But to redeeme a chast and inocent sowle
Forthe from the fierye jawes of lust and hell
Exprest a most comended charity.   190
What second bewtye's that, I intreate you, frend,
That, tremblinge, flyes from his infectious ills
To patronise her youthe and inocence
Beneathe that goode man's goodnes?
   RAPHAEL. Alyke suffers
With her in all distresses, lyke in yeares,   195
In vertue no waye differinge, of our nation;
Who knowes but neare allyde too?
   TREADWAY. I feele somethinge
Growinge on mee, I knowe not howe to style,
Pitty or love, synce it hath tast of boathe.
And since itt weare such parity in all thinges,—   200
Age, minds, wracks, bondadge, pursiutes, injuryes,—
Shoold nowe bee separate? the one be freede,
The tother left in durance for the want
And pious tender of so small a somme?
I somwhat have in purpose.
   RAPHAEL. Dragge them boathe   205
Before the magistrate.
   SARLAB. Mee? wherefore? why?

191 I intreate you] . . . *B.*   197 allyde] all yee *B.*
200 since] sinne *MS. B.*   201 Age] *A correction in MS. for* Years.

GODFREY. As his abetter and ill counseller;
One would have burnt the villadge, and the other
Threatned to fyar the cloyster.

RAPHAEL. Boathe acts capitall
And worthy seveare censure.

MILDEW. Though thou plead'st interest   210
In waye of earnest in Palestra, yet
Robb mee not quite; giue me the tother back,
My only portion left me by the sea
And stock to sett vpp trade by.

SCRIB. Rather torture mee
With any violent death.

TREAD. Leave them in trust   215
And chardge of this grave, reverent gentleman,
Vntill you heire the sentenc of the coort.

ASHB. I willingly accept theire patronadge;
Heere att my howse they shall have meate and harbour,
With all supplyes convenient.

RAPHAELL. Nobly spooke;   220
Meane tyme hale these to th' coort.

MILDEW. My Palestra,
What? not one woord of pittye?

RAPHAEL. Stopp his mouth.

MILDEW. My Scribonia,
Not thou intreate them neather?

TREADWAY. Tyme's but trifled;
Away with them to justyce!

MILDEW. Take my skinne then,   225
Synce nothinge elce is left mee.

220 With . . . convenient.] *Om. B.*
221 th' coort] *A correction in MS. for* justyce.   224 Not] Wilt *B.*

CLOWNE. That's rotten allredy, and will neather make goodd
leather nor parchement. Th' towne theire!

[Exeunt [all except ASHBURNE, PALESTRA, *and*
SCRIBONIA.]

ASHBURNE. Com, damsalls, followe mee where I shall leade.
I have a curst wyfe at home, I tell you that,　　　　　　230
But one that I presume will not bee jealous
Of too such harmeles sowles.

PALESTRA. You are to vs
A patrone and defender.

SCRIB. Bound vnto you
Not as an host but father.　　　　　　　　　*[Exeunt.*

ACTUS TERTIUS

SCENA TERTIA

Enter the LORD DE AVERNE, *his lady,* DENNIS,
and the waytinge mayde.

L. AVERNE. Are all thinges redye as I gave in chardge?
DENYS. Redy, syr.

L. AVERNE. Inoughe; and you deliver'd it
To his owne hands?

MAYDE. I did.

L. AVERNE. Howe did hee tak't?

MAYDE. With smiles and seeminge joy.

L. AVERNE. Sorrowe and shame
I feare will bee the sadd end on't.　　　　　　　　5

228 Th' towne] . . . *B.* [*all except* ASHBURNE, PALESTRA, *and* SCRIBO-
NIA] *Om. B.*　　　　　　　230 curst] cross *B.* (*See note.*)

LADY. Sir, you'r trobled.

LORD AVERNE. I woold not have you so; pray, to your rest.
You shall remove mee from all jelosyes
If you betake you to your sowndest sleepes,
And without more inquiry.

LADY. Sir, remember   10
That all offences are not woorthy deathe:
Fellowny, murder, treason and such lyke
Of that grosse nature maye bee capittall;
Not folly, error, trespasse.

LORD AVERNE. You advyse well;
Lett mee advyse you lyke-wyse: instantly   15
Retyre in to your chamber, without noyse,
Reply, or question, leest part of that rage
Is bent gainst him you turne vpon your self,
Which is not for your safety.

LADY. Syr, good night.   [*Exit.*]
L. AVERNE. How goes the hower?   20
DENIS. 'Tis allmost tenn.

L. AVERNE. The tyme of our appointment. You attend
Vpon his knocks, and giue him free admittans;
Beinge entred, vsher him into this place.
That doon, returne [then] to your ladye's chamber;   25
There locke your self fast in.

MAYDE. My lorde, I shall.—
Poore fryare, I feare they'l putt thee to thy penance
Before they have confest thee.   [*Exit.*]

L. AVERNE. Com, withdrawe;
The watchwoorde's not yet giuen.

Enter the FRYAR *with a letter.*

F. JHON. 'Tis her owne pen. I knewe it, synce shee sett   30

24 vsher] refer *B.*   28 [*Exit.*] *Om. B.*

Her hand to establishe our fowndation;
And, sweete soule, shee hath writt a second tyme
To build mee vpp anewe. *My Lord is ridd*
A three dayes' jorney; loose not this advantadge,
But take tyme by the fore-topp— yes, I will,   35
By the fore-topp and topp-gallant. *At the postorne*
Shee to whose hand you gave your letter, Fryar,
Attends for your dispatch—my busines
I hope shal bee dispatcht then. *Fare you well;*
Fayle mee this night and ever—I'l sooner forfett   40
All pleasures, hopes, preferments, with th' assurance
Of a longe lyfe blest with most happy howers,
Then this one night's contentment.
                    [*Enter* MAYDE.]
  MAYDE. Ha, whoe's theire?
Fryar Jhon?
  F. JHON. The same. You, Mystresse Millisent,
My ladye's gentlewoman?
  MAYDE. I am the closett   45
That treasures all her counsells.
  F. JHON. Is all cleare?
  MAYDE. As such a dark night can bee—to one, I feare,
That scarce will looke on daye more.
  F. JHON. Where's my lady?
  MAYDE. Attends you in her chamber.
  F. JHON. Guide mee too't,
Nay, quickly, guirle—how I allredy surfett   50
In this night's expectation!
  MAYDE. Staye you heare
In this withdraweinge roome; I'l fetch a light

  43 [*Enter* MAYDE.]] *Om. B.*

For safeguard of your shinnes.

    DENIS. Shee might have sayde

For safeguard of his necke.

    MAYDE. My sceane's doon;

The next aᵭ lyes amongst them.   [*Exit.*] 55

    F. JHON. My part dothe but beeginne nowe, and I'l aᵭ it

In exquisite cleane linnen, and this capp

Perfum'd of purpose, least I should smell fryar.

What differ wee i' th' darke, save our shaven crowne,

From gentlemen, nay, lords? Nature hathe arai'd vs   60

As well as the best layemen; why shoold lawe

Restreyne from vs what is allowed to them?

Lett it curbe fooles and idiots, such as througe folly

Will not, or nycenes dare not, tast what's sweete,

Alyke made for all pallats.

    L. AVERNE. Howe the slave   65

Insults in his dam[n]ation! Cease the wretch;

I can indure no longer.

    F. JHON. Such as ban

Proffred delights may, if they please, refuse;

What's borne with mee I will make bold to vse.

    L. AVERNE. And I what thou weart borne too, that's a halter. 70

Pull without feare or mercy; strangle him

With all his sinnes about him. T'were not elce

A revendge woorthe my fury.   [FRY. *strangled.*

    DENNIS. I dare nowe

Lodge him a whole night by my syster's syde;

Hee's nowe past strompettinge.

    L. AVERNE. 'Tis night with him,   75

A longe and lastinge night.

    DENNIS. Hee lyes as quiet.

    58 Perfum'd] Proffred *B.*

You did well, fryare, to putt on your cleane linnen;
'Twill serve you as a shrowde for a new grave.
Whether shall wee lyft his body?

   L. AVERNE. I am on the suddeine
Growne full of thoughts; the horror of the fact   80
Breedes strange seditions in mee.

   DENNIS. Hee perhapps
But conterfetts dead sleep. I'l hollowe to him
To see if I can wake him.

   L. AVERNE. Trifle not;
The sinne will proove more serious. To a consciens
Startled with bloodd and murder, what a terror   85
Is in the deede, beeing doone, which bredd beefore
Boathe a delight and longinge! This sadd spectacle,
Howe itt affrights mee!

   DENNIS. [Lett's remove itt] then.

   L. AVERNE. The sinne it self, the churche's malediction,
As doone to one of a sequestred lyfe   90
And holly order, the lawe's penalty,
Beinge duble forfeture of lyfe and state,
Reproach, shame, infamy, all these incur'd
Through my inconsiderate rashnes!

   DENIS. My lyfe, too.
Howe to prevent the danger of all these?   95

   L. AVERNE. Ey, that will aske much breyne, much project.

   DENIS. Sir,
Shall we poppe him in som privy?

   L. AVERNE. Duble injurye,
To praye vpon the soule and after deathe
Doo to the body such discoortesy;

   84, 85 To . . . murder] *Scored through in MS.*

It neather savours of a generous spyritt   1
Nor that which wee call manly.

    DENIS. Any thinge
For a quiet lyfe, but this same wryneckt death,
That which still spoyles all drinkeinge, 'tis a thinge
I never coold indure; as you are noble,
Keepe still my wind-pype open.

    L. AVERNE. Out of many,   1
Museinge for boath our safetyes, I have fownd
One that's aboue the rest most probable.

    DENIS. What, what, I praye, syr?

    L. AVERNE. Interupt mee not.
Saye I should nowe begett a stratagem
To save myne owne lyf, myne estate and goodds,   1
Ey, and secure thee, too?

    DENIS. 'Twere exellent, syr.

    L. AVERNE. I have projeçt for all these, as willingely
To leng[t]hen boathe our lyves, and limitt vs
Tyme to repent his deathe.

    DENIS. But howe, I praye, syr?

    L. AVERNE. Ey, there's the difficulty—but nowe I hav't.   1
Beetwixt vs and the cloyster's but one wall,
And that of no greate height; coold wee in private
Conveighe this fryar into the monastery,
Itt might bee then imadgin'd som of them
Might bee his deathe's-man; which might seeme more probable1
Bycause, as I had late intelligens,
Theare hathe bin stryfe amongst them.

    DENIS. Better still.

    L. AVERNE. Nowe howe can wee incurr the least suspeçt?

106 Museinge] museings *B. (See note.)*   109 Saye] Staye *B.*

For what should hee doo from the fryary,
Or what make heare att this vnseasoned hower?   125
  DENNIS. I apprehende thee; and, to further this,
In the backe yard there is a ladder, syr:
Mo[u]nt him vpon my back, and I'l conveighe him
Where som, not wee, shall answer for his deathe.
  L. AVERNE. As desperate woonds still must have desperate
    cures,   130
So all rash mischeifes should have suddeine shiftes.
Wee'l putt it to the venter.
  DENNIS. Mount him then;
I'l once trye if the ventur of a ladder
Can keepe mee from the halter.   [*Exeunt.*]

EXPLICIT ACTUS TERTIUS.

124 from the fryary] *A correction in* MS. *for* out of the monastery.
125 make] seeke *B*.   132 the] ye *B*.

ACTUS QUARTUS

SCENA PRIMA

Enter the CLOWNE.

CLOWNE. I have left a full coort behynde mee, Mildewe
pleadinge of the one syde, my mayster on the other, and
the lawyers fendinge and proovinge on boathe; there's
such yeallinge and ballinge, I knowe not whether it made any
deafe to heare it, but I am suer I was almost sicke to see't. Whyle 5
they are brablinge in the cittye, I am sent backe to the villadge
to cheare upp the too yonge mermaydes; for synce theire throates
have bin rincht with salt water, they singe with no lesse sweetenes.
But staye; I spy a fisherman drawinge his nett vpp to the shore;
I'l slacke som of my speede to see howe hee hathe spedd since 10
the last tempest.

Enter the FISHERMAN.

FISHER. I see hee that nought venters, nothinge gaynes;
Hee that will bee awake when others sleepe
May sometymes purchase what maye giue him rest,
When other loyterers shal be forct to ryse   15
Or perish through meeare want; as, for example,
Although the tempest frighted hence the fishe,
I have drag'd some-thinge without finne or skale

12-19 I . . . markett.] *Marked for omission in MS.*

May make mee a good markett. Lett mee better
Surveigh my pryze; 'tis of good weight I feele;   20
Now should it bee some treasure I weare mayde.

CLOWNE. Which if it proove, I'l half marr you or bee half
made with you.

FISHER. Itt must bee gold by th' weight.

CLOWNE. If it bee so heavy, 'tis ten to one but I'l do you the 25
curtesye to ease you of part of your burden.

FISHER. None save my self is guilty of this pryze;
'Tis all myne owne, and I'l beethinke mee best
Howe to beestowe of this ritch magazin.

CLOWNE. And I am stooddinge too with what lyne, what angle, 30
what fisguigge, what castinge nett I can share with you in this
sea booty.

FISHER. I will dissemble, as most ritch men doo,
Pleade poverty and speake my mayster fayre;
By out my freedom for som little soom,   35
And beeinge myne owne man, by lands and hows[es].
That doon, to sea I'l rigge shipps of myne owne,
And synce the sea hathe made mee vpp a stocke,
I'l venter it to sea; who knowes but I
In tyme may proove a noble marchant?   40

CLOWNE. Yes, of eele skinnes.—Staye you, syrrahe!

FISHER. I knowe no fish of that name; limpet, mullett, congar,
dolphin, sharke I knowe and place; I woold som body elce had
thyne; for hearinge, I woold thou hadst none, nor codd; for smelt,
thou art too hott in my nose allredy; but such a fishe cal'd syrra 45
never came within the compasse of my nett. What art thou, a
shrimpe, a dogg-fyshe, or a poore Jhon?

26 part] *A correction in MS. for* half.
41 syrrahe] Syrra, ho *B.*   46 nett] *A correction in MS. for* draught.

CLOWNE. I am one that watcht the tyde to knowe what thou hast caught, and have mony in my pockett to by thy draught.

FISHER. And I am one, thou seest, that have only an empty 50 wett nett, but not so much as the tale of a spratte at thys tyme to sell for love of mony.

CLOW. I grant this is no Fryday, and I at this tyme no cater for the fishemarkett. I only cam to desyre thy judgement and consell.　　　　　　　　　　　　　　　　　55

FISHER. Go to the bench for judgement and to the lawe coorts for consell; I am free of neather, only one of Neptune's poore bastards, a spawne of the sea, and nowe gladly desyres to bee rydd of thee aland.

CLOWNE. Onely one question resolve mee, and I have doone. 60

FISHER. To bee well ridd of thee, I care not if I loose so much tyme.

CLOWNE. But faythefully.

FISHER. As I am honest peeterman.

CLOWNE. Observe mee then:

I saw a theif, comitting fellony;　　　　　　　　　　　　65
I knowe the mayster of the thinge was stolne;
I com vnto this theif, as't might bee thee,
And make this covenant; eather giue mee half,
And make mee sharer, or thou forfettest all;
I'l peach thee to the owner. In this case　　　　　　70
What may I justly claime?

FISHER. Rather then forfett all, I shoold yeild halfe.

CLOWNE. Knowe, then, 'tis thy case, and my case, a most playne case, and concernes the booty in that cap-case. I knowe the lord that wants it and the mayster that owes it; boath howe it was lost 75 and where it was lost. Then come, vnloose, vnbuckle, vnclaspe,

48-54 I . . . fishemarkett.] *Marked for omission in MS.*
66 stolne] *A correction in MS. for* lost.　　76 Then] *Om. B.*

vncase; lett's see what fortne hathe sente vs, and so part it equally beetwixt vs.

FISHER. Staye, staye, my frend; this my case must not be open'd till your case bee better lookt into. Thou knowest who 8 lost it, I who fownd it; thou the lord of it that was, I the owner that nowe is; thou who did possess it, I who doth injoye it; hee had it, I have it; hee migh[t] have kept it, I will keepe it; I venter'd for all, I will inherit all; and there's thy pittifull case layde open.   8

CLOWNE. Fyrst proove this to bee thyne.

FISH. I can and by the fisherman's rethoricke.

CLOWNE. Proceed, sea-gull.

FISHER. Thus, land-spaniell; no man can say this is my fishe till hee finde it in his nett.   9

CLOWNE. Good.

FISHER. What I catche is myne owne, my lands, my goodds, my copy-hold, my fee-simple, myne to sell, myne to giue, myne to lend, and myne to cast away; no man claimes part, no man share, synce fishinge is free and the sea common.   9

CLOWNE. If all bee comon that the sea yeilds, why then is not that as much myne as thyne?

FISHER. By that lawe, when we bringe our fishe to the markett, if every one may freely chuse what hee lykes and take where hee lyst, wee shoold have quicly empty dorsers and cleane 10 stalls, but light purses.

CLOWNE. How canst thou proove that to bee a fishe that was not bredd in the water, that coold never swimme, that hathe neather roe nor milt, scale nor finne, lyfe nor motion? Did ever man heare of a fishe cal'd a budgett? What shape, what collar? 10

FISHER. This shape, this collar; there's rowe within better then

77 see] see then *B*.
96-101] *Marked for omission in MS.*   106 rowe] nowe *B*.

the spawne of sturgeon; I must confesse indeed, they are rare-
ly seene, and seldom fownd; for this is the fyrst I ever catcht in
all the tyme of my fishinge.

CLOWNE. All this sea-sophestry will not serve your turne, for110
where my right is detein'd mee by fayre meanes, I will have it
by force.

FISHER. Of what I caught in the sea?

CLOWNE. Yes, and what I catch hold on ashore. With what consciens canst thou denye mee part of the gaine, when the owner115
hearinge it is in thy custody and within my knowledge, must
eather find mee a principall in the theft, or at least accessary to
the fellony.

FISHER. I'l showe thee a redy waye to prevent boathe.

CLOWNE. Howe that?　　　　　　　　　　120

FISHER. Marry, thus: go thou quietly thy way, I'l go peaca-
bly myne; betraye thou mee to nobody, as I meane to impart
to thee nothinge; seeke thy preferment by land as I have doone
myne by sea; be thou mute, I'l bee dombe; thou silent, I mum-
budgett; thou dismisse mee, I'l acquitte thee; so thou art neath-125
er theife nor accessary.

CLOWNE. Syrrah, though you bee owner of the boate, I'l steare
my course at healme.

FISHER. Hands off, I saye. But hark, a noyse within;
Lett's cease our controversy till wee see　　　[*Noyse within.*130
An end of that.

CLOWNE. Trew, and be judg'd by the next quiet man wee
meete.

FISHER. Content.

Enter, after a noyse, or tumult, ASHBURNE, *his wyfe,*
PALESTRA, SCRIBONIA, *and* GODFREY.

114 ashore] *A correction in MS. for* aland.
120 Howe] How's *B.*　　　　130 *within*] Om. *B.*

WOMAN. I'l not beleeve a sillable thou speak'st.   135
False harts and false toonges go together still;
They boathe are quick in thee.

   ASHBURNE. Have patience, woman.

   WOMAN. I have bin too longe a grizell. Not content
To have thy hawnts abroad, where theire are marts
And places of lewd brothelry inough   140
Wheare thou mai'st wast thy body, purse, and creditt,
But thou woold'st make thy private howse a stewes!

   ASHB. But heare mee, wyfe.

   WOMAN. I'l heare none but myselfe.
Are your legges growne so feeble on the suddeine
They fayle when you shoold travell to your whoores,   145
But you must bringe them home and keepe them heare
Vnder my nose? I am not so past my sences
But at this age can smell your knavery.

   PALESTRA. Good woman, heare's none such.

   WOMAN. Bold baggadge, peace!
'Tis not your turne to prate yet; lust and impudens   150
I knowe still goe together. Showes itt well
In one that's of thy yeares and gravity,
That ought to bee in lyfe and government
To others an example, nowe to doate
So neere the grave, to walke beefore his doore   155
With a yonge payer of strompetts at his tale!
Naye, make his honest and chast wyfe no better
Then a madam makareele!

   GODFREY. Why, this storme's woorse then that vntil'd the
     howse!

   ASHBURNE. But vnderstand mee: 160

151-158 Showes . . . makareele!] *Marked for omission in MS.*
154 an] and *MS.*

Itt is meare pitty and no bad intent,
No vnchast thought but my meare charity
In the remembrans of our longe lost child,
To showe som love to these distressed maydes.
   WOMAN. Sweete charity! Nay, vsury withall!   165
For one chyld lost, whose goodnes might have blest
And bin an honor to our family,
To bringe mee home a cuple of loose thinges!
I knowe not what to terme them, but for thee,
Owld fornicator, that jad'st mee att home   170
And yet can find a yonge colt's toothe abroad,
Ould as I am, myne eyes are not so dimme
But can discerne this without spectacles.
Hence from my gate, you syrens com from sea,
Or as I lyve I'l washe your paintinges off,   175
And with hotte skaldinge water instantly.   [*Exit.*
   GODFREY. Nay then, sweet-harts, you canott staye; you
have had could interteinment.
   PALESTRA. The land's to vs as dreadfull as the seas,
For wee are heare, as by the billowes, tost   180
From one feare to another.
   ASHBURNE. Prety sowles,
Despyer not you of comfort; I'l not leave you
To the least danger till som newes returne
From him that vndertakes your patronadge.
You, syrrah, vsher them vnto the fryeary,   185
Whence none dares force them. I have a curst wyf you see,
And better you then I take sanctuary.
   SCRIBON. Wee will bee sweyde by you as one in whome
Wee yet have fownd all goodnes.

164 maydes] maydens *B.*   171 find] fend [?] *B.*
186 curst] cross *B.*

ASHBUR. Leave them theire
To safety; then returne.   19

[*Exeunt* PALESTRA, SCRIBONIA, *and* GODFREY.]
CLOWNE. What say'st thou to this gentleman?
FISHER. No man better.—Now it will go on my syde; this
is my owne mayster, suer hee cannott bee so vnaturall to giue
sentens against his owne naturall servant.—Syr, good daye.
ASHBURNE. Gramercyes, I in troth much suffered for thee,19
Knowinge howe rashly thou expos'd thy self
To such a turbulent sea.
CLOWYNE. I lykewyse, syr, salute you.
ASHB. Thanks, good frend.
CLOWNE. But, syr, is this your servant?
FISHER. Yes, syrrahe, and this my mayster.   20
CLOWNE. Then I have nothinge at this tyme to doo with thee.
FISHER. Marry, a good motion; farewell and bee hangde.
CLOWNE. Wee are not so easily parted. —Is this your man?
ASHBURNE. Yes, I acknowledge him;
And thou I thinke beelongst to Mr. Raphael,   20
Imployde about these women?
CLOWNE. Yes, I acknowledge it; but you are suer hee's yours?
ASHBURNE. Once againe I doo confesse him myne.
CLOWNE. Then heare mee speake.
FISHER. Heare mee, your servant, fyrst.
[ASHBURNE.] Say, what's the stryfe?
CLOWNE. Marry, who fyrst shall speake.   21
FISHER. That's I.
CLOWNE. I appeale then to the curtesy due to a stranger.

190 [*Exeunt* . . . GODFREY]] *Ext. ma: Ashb. MS. B.*
200-203] *Marked for omission in MS.*   200 this my] *thy B.*
209-213 fyrst . . . servant.] *Marked for omission in MS. and replaced by* what
ere . . . .   209 fyrst] *Om. B.*

FISHER. And I to the right belonginge to a howshou[ld] servant.

ASHBUR. I'l heare the stranger fyrst.

CLOWNE. In this you doo but justyce. I pray tell mee,—215
[y]ou vente[r on the] sea,—is this a fishe or no? Or, if a fishe,
what fishe do you call it? (Peace, you.)

ASHBUR. It is no fishe nor fleshe.

CLOWNE. Nor good redd herringe—fisherman, y'are gone.

FISHER. Thou art deceav'd; I am heare still, and may have220
heare for ought I knowe to by all the redd herringe in Marcell[is].

CLOWNE. Did you ever heare of a fishe cal'd a budgett?

ASHBUR. I protest never synce I knew the sea.

CLOWNE. You are gone againe, fisherman.   225

FISHER. I am heare still; and, nowe, master, heare mee.

CLOWNE. Lett mee proceed. This bagge, this knappsacke, or
this portmantua hee woold make a fishe bycause tooke in his
nett. Nowe, syr, I com to you with this ould proverbe: all's not
fishe that coms. to nett.—There you are, gone agayn.   230

FISHER. But—

CLOWNE. No butt, nor turbutt. I suspect this budgett to be the
bawde's, in which are the discoveryes of this yonge woman's
coontry and parents. Nowe, syr, for their sakes, for my mayster's sake, for all our sakes vse the authority of a mayster to235
searche, and showe the power you have over a servant to com-
and.

                    [*Enter* GODFREY.]

ASHBUR. Will hee or not, hee shall assent to that.

FISHER. A meere trick to vndoo mee, ere I knowe what I
am wanting.   240

213 howshou[ld] servant]. . . what ere he says *B.*
216 [y]ou vente[r on the]] . . . *B.*   233 are the] are the the *MS.*
237 [*Enter* GODFREY.]]*Om. B.*   239 FISHER] CLOWNE *MS. B.*

ASHB. Call in the damseles;
Intreate them fayrely heather. Say wee hope
We shall have good newes for them.   [*Exit* GODFREY.]

FISHER. I will part with it only on this condition, that if there
bee nothinge in it which concernes them, the rest may returne₂
to mee vnrifled and vntutcht.

ASHB. Did it conteyne the valew of a myne
I clayme no part in it.

FISH. Nor you?

CLOWNE. Nor I.

FISHER. By the contents of this budgett.

CLOWNE. I sweare.

ASHB. I vowe.

FISHER. Then there, tak't to you, mayster, and once more₂
good luck on my syde!

   Enter GODFREY, *vsheringe in* PALESTRA *and* SCRIBONIA.

PALEST. You sent to speake with vs?

ASHB. I did indeed;
Saye, knowe you this? Y'have leave, surveigh it well.

PALESTRA. This? knowe I this? Oh, my Scribonia, see!
Yes, and by this alone may knowe my self.   2
Looke well vpon't, deare syster. Extasy
May dimme myne eyes; it canot purblind thyne.

SCRIB. Itt is the same, Palestra.

FISHER. Then suer I shall not bee the same man in the after-
noone that I was in the morninge.   2●

SCRIBO. In this is a greate masse of wealthe included,
All that the bawde hathe by corruption gott
In many a thrifty yeare.

FISHER. Comfort for mee.

ASHBUR. But tell mee, is there ought of yours included,

  243 [*Exit* GODFREY.]] *Om. B.*

Which you may justly chalendge?

PALESTRA. Of that gould,　　　265
No not the valewe of one poor deneere:
'Tis all base brokadge boath of sinne and shame
Of which wee neare weare guilty; yet inclosed
There shall you find a cabinet of myne,
Where boathe my naturall parents you may see　　　270
In a small roome intruded.

FISHER. An vnatrall child thou art to thrust thy naturall parents into a leatheren bagge and leave them in the bottom of y^e
sea.

PALEST. Showe mee the caskett; if beefore you ope it　　　275
I do not name you every parcell in't,
Lett it no more be myne; mak't your owne pryse.
But such small trifles as I justly chalenge
And canott yeild you the least benefitt,
Of them lett mee bee mystresse, synce they are　　　280
The somme and crowne of all my future hopes,
But from my tender infancy detein'd.
As for the gould and jewells, make't your spoyle;
Of that I clayme no portione.

FISHER. I accept of the condition.

ASHBURNE. Itt is boathe just and honest; i'th' meane tyme, 285
Virgin, stand you aloofe; wee'l have no juggling.
And, Gripus, synce the busines concernes you,
Have you a curious ey too't.

FISHER. Feare not mee, for boathe at sea and land I was ever
a goodd marksman.　　　290

ASHBUR. The caskett is nowe open'd; what coms fyrst?

PALEST. Aboue, the clothes in which I fyrst was swathde,

271 intruded] intended *B.*　　　272 thrust] trust *B.*
285, 286 i'th' . . . aloofe] *Om. B.*

The linnen fyrst worne in myne infancy.

ASHBUR. These are child's swathinges; whether thyne or no
It is to mee vncerteine. To the rest! 295

PALESTR. And next to these is a ritche handkercher,
Where you shall find in golden letters wrought
My place of byrthe, myne and my father's name.

ASHB. Heare's such a handkercher, such letters workt;
Speake them, as I shall reade them.

PALEST. Mirable. 300

ASHB. Right! Myrable.

PALESTRA. Doughter of Jhon Ashburne, marchant.

ASHBURNE. Trewe: of Jhon Ashburne, marchant.—Oh my
sowle!
—Proceed, prithee proceede.

PALESTRA. And borne in Christ-chyrch, London, Anno—

ASHB. 1530. 305
Oh you imortall powers. I stagger yet
Beetwixt dispayer and hope, and canott guesse
Which waye my fate will swaye mee; oh speake, speake!
Thy mother's name?

PALEST. Reade it in sylver letters playnly wrought 310
In the next imbrodered linnen.

ASHB. If that fayle not,
I then have a firme rock to build vpon.—
The guift of Isabell to her doughter, Mirable.—
Oh frend, oh servant!

CLOWNE. Howe is't, syr?

FISHER. How now, mayster?

ASHB. I that so many yeares have bin despoyl'd, 315
Neclected, shattered, am made vpp againe,
Repaired, and new created.

PALESTRA. Search but further
And there's a golden brooch in it, a diamond,
Vpon my byrthday giuen mee by my father.

ASHBU. I have longe sought and nowe at lengthe have found 320
That diamond, thee my doughter.

PALESTRA. How, syr?

ASHBUR. Shee that so late excluded thee my howse
And shutt these gates against thee, Isabell,
Thy mother, these weare her owne handyworkes
Beestowde vpon thee in thyne infancy   325
To make vs nowe boathe happy in thy groath.
I am Jhon Ashburne, marchant, London, Christ Church;
The yeare, place, tyme agree thee to bee myne,
Oh mirhor of thy sex, my Myrable!

PALEST. This surplusadge of joy should not bee feign'd.   330

ASHB. No more then these noates are infallible.

PALEST. Thus then in all humility I kneele
To you my acknowledg'd father.

ASHB. Ryse, my guirle.

FISHER. Had I not drawne this leiward [?] out of the sea, where
had it bin? All drownd by this.   335

ASHB. No triflinge nowe; post, Godfrey, to my wyfe.
Tell her no more then thou hast heard and seene.
Shee's hard of faythe; relate it pu[n]ctually.
Beare her (oh lett mee borrowe them so longe)
These better to confirme her; bid her hast,   340
And for the truth add these as testimony—
Nay, art thou heare still?

GODFREY. Lyke a shadowe vanisht,
But to returne a substance.   [*Exit.*]

326 groath] yoouth *B.*   330 feign'd] forged *B.*
343 [*Exit.*]] [*Exit* GODFREY. *B.*

ASHB. Oh, my deare doughter!—where's yong Raphael's man?
Beare him of all what thou hast seene a perfect   34
And trew relation.

CLOWNE. Ey, syr.

ASHB. Bidd him, too,
All business sett apart, make hether

CLOWNE. Ey, syr.

ASHB. Tell him that his Palestra is my Mirable.

CLOWNE. Ey, syr.

ASHB. And that shee is my doughter, my lost child.   35

CLOWNE. Ey, syr.

ASHB. And that of all this I am most assur'd.

CLOWNE. Ey, syr.

ASHB. Thou wilt not doo all this?

CLOW. I will; you lye, syr.

ASHB. Howe, syr?   35

CLOW. Ey, syr.

ASHB. Say that this daye shee shal be made his wyfe.

CLOWNE. Ey, syr.

ASHB. Why then add winges vnto your heeles and fly, syr.

CLOWNE. Ay, syr, but ere I take my flight, for this good serv-36
yce,
You'l mediate with him for my freedom?

ASHBUR. So.

CLOWNE. And woo your doughter to doo so too?

ASH. So.

CLOWNE. And saye to him I shal be thankefull.

ASH. So.

CLOWNE. Your doughter's and your servant ever.

ASHB. So.   36

CLOWNE. To go, roonne, ryde of all your arrants.

364 saye] syr *B.*   365 your] your your *MS.*

ASH. So.

CLOWNE. In all this you'l bee slack in nothinge?

ASH. So.

CLOWNE. And you'l heareafter love mee still?

ASHB. So, so.

CLOWNE. Howe, but so, so?

ASHB. Yes, so and so and so.

CLOWNE. Why, then I go, go, goe.   [*Exit.*]370

ASHBU. But one thinge I intreate you, Mirable:

This thyrteene yeares, synce by rude creditors

Tost and opprest, naye rent out of myne owne,

I have bin forc̓t to seeke my fate abroad,

Howe weare you ravisht thence, or since that tyme   375

What strange adventures past?

　　　Enter GODFREY *and the wyf, with the handkerch*[*er.*]

MIRABLE. My mother's presence

Must now prevent my answer.

WYFE. Where is shee? oh wheare, wheare? For by these tok-
　　ens,

These of her childhood, most vnfallid signes,

I knowe her for my doughter.

MIRABLE. I have bin   380

The longe and wretched owner of that cabinet

With all therein contein'd.

WIFE. Into thy boosom

Oh lett mee rayne a shower of joyfull teares

To welcom thee, my Mirable.

GODFREY. You threatned her but nowe with skaldinge water;385

mee thinks you had more neede to comfort her with hott waters,

for suer shee canott bee warme synce shee came so late out of the

could bathe.

　　370 [*Exit.*]] [*Exit* CLOWN. B.

WYF. Make fyares, bid them make ready wholesom brothes,
Make warme the bedd, and see the sheetes well ayred.   39
Att lengthe then have I fownd thee?

ASHB. But what's shee
That's in thy fellow-shippe?

MIRABLE. My fellowe sharer
In all misfortunes; and for many yeares
So deere to mee, I canot tast a blessednes
Of which shee's not partaker.

WYF. For thy sake   39
Shee shall bee myne too, and (in her) I'l thinke
The powers aboue have for my single losse
Giuen mee at lengthe a duble recompence.

SCRIBO. For which hee that protects all inocence
Will in good tyme reward you.

WYFE. Praye, in, in;   40
This could is prejuditiall to your healthes.
I'l count you boathe my twinnes.

[*Exeunt* [WIFE, PALESTRA, *and* SCRIBONIA.]

ASH. Strange alteration!
Skoldinge is turn'd to pitty, spleen and mallyce
To mercye and compassion.

FISHER. But your promisse tutchinge my budgett?   40
ASHB. Godfreye, beare it in
And lodge it safe; there's nowe no tyme for that;
Wee'l talke of it herafter.

GODFREY. Fellowe Gripus, I am made for this tyme porter.
Ladeys, your trusty treasurer.   41

[*Exeunt* [ASHBOURNE *and* GODFREY.]

GRIPUS. These are the fishermen, and I the fishe catcht in the

402 *Exeunt*] *Exit MS. Ext. B.*   407 nowe] *Om. B.*
410 *Exeunt*] *Exit MS. Ext. B.*

nett; well my comfort is, though my booty have made mee no
ritcher then I was, poorer then I am I canott bee. Nowe wherin
is the ritche more happy then the poore? I thinke rather lesse
blessed, and that shall appeare by this exellent good ballet,415
though sett to a scurvy tune.

Lett ech man speake as he's possest;
I hold the poore man's state most blest.
For if longe lyfe contentment breedes,
In that the poore the ritche exceedes; 420
 The ritch man's dayes are short, as spent
In pleasures and supposed content;
Whylest to vs poore men care and troble
Makes every hower wee wast seeme duble.

He that hathe ech daye to his backe 425
Chandge of gaye suites, whylst wee, alacke,
Have but one coate, that coorse and ould,
Yet it defends vs from the could;
 As warme, too, in an equll eye
As they in all theire purple dye; 430
'Mongst all theire store, they weare, wee see,
But one att onc, and so do wee.

The ritch that at his table feasts
With choyse of dayntyes, sundry guests,
In all his plenty can but fill 435
On[e] belly; so the poore can still
 With cheese and onions, and disguest
As well with them as th' others feast.
The pesent with his homespoon lasse
As many merry howers may passe 440

413-416 Nowe . . . . tune.] *Marked for omission in* MS.
415 appeare] approue *B.*
417-446] *Apparently marked for omission in* MS.

As coortiers with there sattin guirles,
Though ritchly deckt in gould and pearles;
And, though but playne, to purpose wooe,
Nay oft tymes with lesse danger too.
And yet for all this I have one crotchett left in my pate to bate 445
a new hooke for the gold in the portmantua.   [*Exit.*]

ACTUS QUARTUS

SCENA SECUNDA

Enter DENNIS, *with the* FRYAR, *from aboue, vpon his backe.*

DENNIS. Whether a knavishe or a sinnefull load,
  Or one ore boathe, I knowe not; massye it is,
And if no frend will for mee, I'll bee sorry
For myne owne heavinesse. And heare's a place,
Though neather of the secretest nor the best,   5
To vnlade my self of this iniquity.
When I satt late astryde vpon the wall,
To lyft the ladder this waye for descent,
Mee thought the fryar lookt lyke S. George a horsbacke,
And I his trusty steede. But nowe's no triflynge: 10
Hee's where hee is in commons, wee dischardg'd,
Boathe of suspect and murther; which lett the covent
To-morrow morninge answer howe they cann.
I'l back the waye wee came; what's doon, none sawe
I' th' howse nor heare; they answer then the lawe.   15
                [*Exit.*

445 pate] fate *B.*   SCENA SECUNDA] Scena 3a *MS. B.*
3 will for mee] *A correction in MS. for* at this tyme.
13 howe they cann] *A correction in MS. for* for my guest[?].
15 heare] herde *B.*   lawe] Lawyer *B.*

Enter FRYAR RICHARD.

F. RICH. Of all infirmityes belonginge to vs
I hould those woorst that will not lett a man
Rest in his bedd a-nights. And I of that,
By reason of a late could I have gott,
Am at this instant gulty; which this rysinge　　　20
From a warme bedd in these could, frosty nights
Rather augments then helpes; but all necessityes
Must bee obey'd. But soft, there's one before mee;
By this small glimps of moone-light I perceave him
To bee Fryar Jhon, my antient adversary.　　　25
Why, Jhon? why, brother? what? not speake? Nay, then,
I see 'tis doon of mallyce, and of purpose
Only to shame mee, since hee knowes the rest
Take notyce what a loose man I am growne.
Nay, prithee, sweete Fryar Jhon, I am in hast,　　　30
Horrible hast; doo but release mee nowe,
I am thy frend for ever. What! not heare!
Feigne to bee deaf of purpose, and of slight!
Then heare is that shall rowse you. Are you falne?
　　　[*Eather strykes him with a staffe or casts a stone.*
What, and still mute and sylent? nay, not styrr?　　　35
I'l rowse you with a vengance! not one limbe
To doo his woonted offyce, foot nor hand?
Not a pulse beatinge, no breathe? what, no motion?
Oh mee of all men lyvinge most accurst!
I have doon a fearefull murder, which our former　　　40
Inveterate hate will be a thousand testats
That I for that insidiated his lyfe.
The deede's apparant, and the offens past pardon.

20 rysinge] rushinge *B.*　　　21 could] wild *B.*
26 brother] Jhon *B.*　　Nay] why *B.*

There's nowe no way but fly. But fly! Which way?
The cloyster gates are all bar'd and fast lockt;   4
These suddeine mischeifes should have suddeine shifts.
About it brayne and in good tyme. I ha'te!
Suspitious r[u]mors have bin lately spread
And more then whispered of th' incontinent love
Fryar Jhon boare the knight's lady. Had I meanes   5
Howe to conveighe his body ore the wall
To any or the least part of the howse,
It might bee thought the knight in jelosy
Had doon this murder in a just revendge.
Let me surveighe th' ascent: happy occation!   5
To see howe redy still the devill is
To helpe his servants! Heare's a ladder left:
Vpp, Fryare, my purpose is to admitt you nowe
Of a newe cloyster. I will sett his body
Vpright in the knight's porche and leave my patron   6
To answer for the falt, that hathe more strength
Then I to tugge with benshes.

                          [*Exit. Carry him vp.*
   Enter the KNIGHT, *half vnredy, his* LADY *after him.*
   D'AVERNE. Ho, Dennis!
   LADY. Giue mee reason, I intreate,
Of these vnquiet sleepes.
   D'AVERNE. You dogg mee, lady,
Lyke an ill genius.
   LADY. You weare woont to call mee   65
Your better angell.
   D'AVERNE. So I shall doo still,
Would you beetake you to your quiet sleepes
And leave mee to my wakeinges.

    50 boare] boare to *B.*

LADY. There beelonges
Vnto one bedd so sweete a sympathy,
I canott rest without you.
  D'AVERNE. To your chamber!   70
There may growe elce a worse antypathy
Betwixt your love and myne; I tell you, lady,
Myne is no woman's busines. No reply!
Your least inforced presence att this tyme
Will but begett what you would loathe to beare, 75
Quarrell and harshe vnkindnes.
  LADY. Ever your lipps
Have bin too mee a lawe. — I suspect more
Then I woold apprehend with willingenes;
But though prevention canott helpe what's past,
Conjugall faythe may expresse it self at last. *[Exit.]* 80
  D'AVERNE. Why, Denis. Ho! Awake and ryse in hast!
     [Enter DENIS.]
  DENIS. What, is your lordshipp madd?
  D'AVERNE. Knowest thou what's past
And canst thou skape this danger?
  DENIS. Did I not tell you
That all was safe, the body too disposed
Better then in his grave?
  D'AVERNE. Strange thoughts sollicite mee. 85
Vpp and inquire about the cloyster wall
What noyse thou hearest, if any pryvate whisperinge
Or lowder vprore 'bout the murder ryse.
  DENIS. I shall, I shall, syr.   *[Exit.]*
  D'AVERNE. Guilt, thoughe it weare a smoothe and peace-
   full face,   90

74 inforced] insured *B.*   80 *[Exit.]*] *[Exit Lady. B.*
81 *[Enter* DENIS.]] *Om. B.* 89 *[Exit.]*] *[Exit Dennis. B.*

Yet is within full of seditious thoughts
That makes continuall faction.   [*Exit.*

Enter FRYAR RICHARD, *with* FRYAR JHON *vpon his
backe.*

F. RICHARD. This is the porch that leades into the hall;
Heare rest for thyne and myne owne better ease.
This hauing doon, to prevent deathe and shame,   95
By the same stepps I'l back the waye I came.

[FRYER *sett vp & left. Exit.*
Enter DENIS, *half vnredy.*

DENIS. This is the penalty beelonges to servyce:
Masters still plott to theire owne pryvate ends
And wee that are theire slaves and ministers
Are cheif still in the troble; they ingrosse   100
The pleasure and the profitt, and wee only
The swett and payne. My lord hathe doon a mischiefe,
And nowe I must not sleepe for't. What art thou?
None of the howse suer, I should knowe thy face then:
Beesydes my lord giues no such lyvery.   105
Nowe in the name of heaven, what art thou? Speake,
Speake if thou beest a man! or, if a ghost,
Then glyde hence lyke a shadowe! 'Tis the——oh!——
The fryar hathe nimbly skipt back ore the wall,
Hath lyke a surly justyce bensht himself,   110
And sitts heare to accuse vs! Where's my lord?
Helpe, helpe! His murdered ghost is com from hell
On earthe to cry, "Vindicta!"

Enter L. D'AVERNE.

D'AVERNE. What clamor's this?
DENIS. Oh, syr——

92 faction] follie *B.*
103 for't] *Om. B.*   109 ore] over *B.*

D'AVERN. Why, howe is't, Denis?

DENIS. Never woorse—the fryar, syr—

D'AVERNE. What of him?   115

DENIS. The slave that would not leave the place but carried,
Is of him self com back.

D'AVERNE. Whether?

DENIS. Looke theire.

D'AVERNE. That which I took to bee meare fantasy
I finde nowe to bee real; murder is
A cryinge sinne, and canott be conceal'd.   120
Yet his returne is strange.

DENNIS. 'Tis most prodigious;
The very thought of it hath putt a creeke
Into my necke allredy.

D'AVERN. One further desperate tryall I will make
And putt it to adventer.

DENNIS. Pray how's that, syr?   125

D'AVERNE. There's in my stable an ould stallion, once
A lusty horse but nowe past servyce.

DENNIS. Goodd, syr.

D'AVERNE. Him I'l have sadled and capparrison'd.
Heare in the hall a rusty armor hanges,
Pistolls in rotten cases, an ould sword,   130
And a cast lance, to all these sutable.
I'l have them instantly tooke downe.

DENNIS. And then?

D'AVER. In these I'l arme the fryar from head to knee,
Mount him into his saddle, with stronge cords
There bind him fast, and to his gantlet hand   135
Fasten his lance. For basses, 'tis no matter;
These his grey skyrts will serve. Thus arm'd, thus mo[u]nted,

127 Goodd] Godd *MS. B.*

Turne him out of the gates, neither attended
With squire or page, lyke a stronge knight adventers   140
To seeke a desperate fortune.

    DENIS. Hee may so if hee please
Ryde post vnto the devill.

    D'AVERNE. This I'l see doone;
'Tis a decree determinde.

    DENIS. Capp a pe
I'l see him arm'd and mo[u]nted.   [*Exeunt.* 145

            Enter FRYAR RICHARD.

    F. RICH. This murder canott bee so smoothred vpp
But I in th' end shall paye for't; but feare still
Is wittye in prevention. Nowe for instance
There's but one refuge left mee; that's to fly:
The gates are shutt vpon mee, and my self   150
Am a badd foott-man, yet these difficultyes
I can thus helpe; there to this place belonges
A mare that every second daye's imployde
To carry corne and fetch meale from the mill,
Distant som half league off; I by this beast   155
Will fashion myne escape.—What, baker, ho!

    BAKER (*within*). What's hee that calls so early?

            [*Enter* BAKER.]

    F. RICHARD. I, Fryar Richard.

    BAKER. What would you have that you are stirringe thus
An hower beefore the dawne.

    F. RICHARD. I canott sleepe,
And vnderstandinge there's meale redy grownd,   160
Which thou must fetch this morninge from the mill,
I'l save thee so much pay[n]es. Lend mee the beast,
And lett mee forthe the gate; I'l bringe boathe back

    157 [*Enter* BAKER.]] *Om. B.*

Ere the bell ringe to mattens.

  BAKER. Marry, Fryar Ritchard,

With all my hart, and thanke yee. I'l but ryse   165

And halter her, then lett you forthe the gate;

You'l save mee so much labour.

  F. RICHARD. This falls out

As I coold wishe, and in a fort[u]nate hower;

For better then to too legges trust to fower.   [*Exeunt.*]

EXPLICIT ACTUS QUARTUS

  164 to] for *B.*   169 [*Exeunt*]] *Om. B.*

ACTUS QUINTUS

SCENA PRIMA

Enter THOMAS ASHBURNE, *the yonger brother to Jhon,*
a merchant, with one of his factors.

THOMAS. Are all thinges safe abord?

    FACTOR. As you can wishe, sir;
And notwithstandinge this combustious stryfe
Betwixt the winds and seas, our shipp still tight,
No anchar, cable, tackle, sayle, or mast
Lost, thoughe much danger'd; all our damadge is   5
That, where our purpose was for Italy,
We are driven into Marcellis.

    THOMAS. That's myne vnhappines
That, beinge bound vpon a brother's quest
Longe absent from his country, who of late
After confinement, penury, distresse   10
Hathe gain'd a hopefull fortune, and I travelling
To beare him tydinges of a blest estate,
Am in my voyadge thwarted.

    FACTOR. In what province
Resydes hee att this present?

    THOMAS. His last letters
That I receav'd weare dated from Leagahorne;   15

   his factors] *the Factors B.*
   1 *(marginal stage directions in another hand)*] Fact: Gibson. *MS.*
   8 bound] come *B.*

Nowe wee by this infort[u]nate storme are driven
Into Marcellis roads.

FACTOR. For the small tyme
Of our abode heare what intend you, sir?

THOMAS. To take in victuall and refresh our men,
Provyde vs of thinges needefull, then onc more   20
With all the expeditious hast wee can
Sett sayle for Florens.

FACTOR. Please you, sir,
I'l steward well that busines.

THOMAS. I' th' meane tyme
I shall find leisure to surveigh the town,   25
The keyes, the temples, forts, and monuments;
For what's the end of travell but to better vs
In judgment and experiens? What are these?
Withdrawe and giue them streete-roome.

      Enter RAPHAEL, TREADEWAY, *and the* CLOWNE.

RAPHAEL. Hath my Palestra fownd her parents then?   30
CLOWNE. As suer as I had lost you.
RAPHAEL. And free borne?
CLOW. As any in Marcellis.
RAPHAEL. Englishe, say'st thou?
CLOWNE. Or Brittishe, which you please.
RAPHAEL. Her trew name Mirable
And Ashburne's dougter?

CLOWNE. Suer as yours is Raphael
And Treadwaye's his.   35

THOMAS. Mirable and Ashburne!
FACTOR. Names that concerne you, sir.
THOMAS. Peace, listen farther.
RAPHAEL. Thou with these woords hast extasyde my sowle,

34 Raphael] Raphaels *MS. B.*

And I am all in rapture. Then hee's pleas'd
Wee too shal be contracted?

 CLOWNE. 'Tis his mynd, sir.   40
 RAPHAEL. The moother, too, consents?
 CLOWNE. So you shall finde, sir.
 RAPHAEL. And Mirable pleas'd, too?
 CLOWNE. Shee's so inclin'd, sir.
 RAPHAEL. And this the very day?
 CLOWNE. The tyme assign'd, sir.
 RAPHAEL. Shee shal be suerly myne.
 CLOWNE. As vowes can bind, sir.
 RAPHAEL. Thou sawest all this?
 CLOWNE. I am suer I was not blind, sir. 45
 RAPHAEL. And all this shall bee doon?
 CLOWNE. Beefore you have din'd, sir.
 RAPHAEL. Oh, frend, eather pertake with mee in joy
And beare part of this surplus; I shall elce
Dye in a pleasinge surfett.

 TREADWAY. Frend, I doo
Withall intreate you interceade for mee   50
To your fayre love's companion, for if all
Th' estate I have in France can by her freedom,
Shee shall no longer faynt beneathe the yoake
Of lewdnes and temptation.

 RAPHAEL. The extent
Of that fyxt love I ever vowde to the   55
Thou in this act shall find.

 TREADWAY. And it shall seale it,
Beyond all date or limitt.

 RAPHAELL. Com, hasten, frend; mee thinks at leng[t]he I spy
After rough tempests a more open skye.

     [*Exeunt* RAPHAEL *and* TREADWAY.]

CLOWNE. And I will after you, kind syr, 60
Since so merrily blowes the wind, sir.

THOMAS. Staye, frend, I am a stranger in these parts
And woold in one thinge gladly bee resolv'd.

CLOWNE. I am in hast.

THOMAS. That little leasure thou beestowest on mee 65
I shal bee gladd to paye for; nay, I will.
Drinke that for my sake.

CLOWNE. Not this, syr, as it is; for I can make a shift to dissolve
hard mettall into a more liquid substans. A cardeq? Oh, syr, I
can distill this into a quintessens cal'd argentum potabile. 70

THOMAS. I heard you name one Ashburne; can you bring mee
To th' sight of such a man?

CLOWNE. Easily I can, syr. But for another peice of the same
stampe, I can bringe you to heare him, to feele him, to smell [him],
to tast him, and to feede vpon him your whole fyve sences. 75

THOMAS. There's for thee, though I have no hope at all
To finde in France what I in Florens seeke.
And though my brother have no child alyve,
As longe sy[n]ce lost when I was rob'd of myne,
Yet for the name-sake, to my other travells 80
I'l add this little toyle, though purposeles.
I have about mee letters of import
Dyrected to a marchant of that name
For whose sake (beeinge one to mee intyred)
I only crave to see the gentleman. 85

CLOWNE. Beleeve mee, syr, I never love to jest with those that
beeforehand deale with mee in earnest. Will you followe mee?

THOMAS. Proove hee my brother, and his daughter fownd,
Lost by my want of care (which canott bee,

60 kind] home *B.*   74 [him]] *Om. B.*
86 that] that that *MS.*   88 Proove] Prooves *B.*

All reasons well considered), and I so happy   90
To bringe him newes of a recovered state,
Who to his foes so longe hathe bin a pray,
I'd count my monthes and years but from this day.

       [*Exeunt.*

ACTUS QUINTUS

SCENA SECUNDA

Enter att one doore D'AVERNE, *and* DENNIS *with the fryar
armed, at the other* FRYAR RICHARD *and the* BAKER.

D'AVERNE. So nowe all's fitt, the daylight's not yet broake;
   Mount him and lock him in the saddle fast,
Then turne him forthe the gates.

    DENIS. Pray, syr, your hand to rayse him.

    D'AVERNE. Nowe lett him post whether his fate shall guide
   him.   [*Exeunt.*] 5

    BAKER. The mare's ready.

    F. RICH. Only the key to ope the cloyster gate;
Then all is as it shoold bee.

    BAKER. Tak't; there 'tis.
But make hast, good Fryar Richard; you will elce
Have no new bredd to dinner.

    F. RICH. Feare not, baker;   10
I'l proove her mettall. Thus I back one mare
Least I shoold ryde another.   [*Exit.*

    BAKER. It is the kindest novyce of my consciens
That ere woare hood or coole.

       [*A noyse within. Trampling of horses.*
What noyse is that? Now by the Abbot's leave   15
I will looke out and see.   [*Exit.*]

5 *Ent.* RICH., BAKER.] *B. MS. (in later hand).*
16 [*Exit.*]] [*Clere. MS. (in later hand). B.*

Enter AVERNE *and* DENNIS.

D'AVERN. Howe nowe? the newes?
The cause of that strange vprore?
   DENNIS. Strange indeed,
But what th' event will bee, I canott guess.
   D'AVERNE. Howe is it? Speake.
   DENNIS. I had no sooner, as your lordshipp badd,   2•
Putt him vpon his voyadge, turn'd him out,
But the ould resty stallion snuft and neigh'd,
And smelt, I thinke, som mare, backt (I perceav'd
By th' moone light) by a fryar, in whose pursuite
Our new made horsman with his threatninge lance,   2
Pistolles, and rotten armor made such noyse
That th' other, frighted, clamours through the streetes
Nothinge but deathe and murder.
   D'AVERN. But the sequell?
The clamour still increasethe.   [*Noyse.*

Enter the BAKER *rooninge.*

   BAKER. Oh never, never,
Was seene such open mallyce!
   DENNIS. What's the busines?   3•
   BAKER. Giue mee but leave to breath—oh, especially in a
   cloyster?
   DENNIS. Out wee't, man.
   BAKER. The novyce Richard, to save mee a labour,
Borrowed my mare to fetch meale from the mill.
I knowe not howe the devill Fryar Jhon knew't,   3
But all in armor watcht him goinge out
And after spurrs to chardge him, beinge vnarm'd;
& suer if hee canott reatch him with his lance,
Hee'l speede him with his pistolls.

   24 th'] the *B.*   34 from] for *B.*   38 &] O *B.*

DENNIS. All's well yet. [*Noyse.*

BAKER. This noyse hath cal'd much people from there bedds, 40
And trobled the whole villadge.

FR. RICH. (*within.*) Hold, hold, I do confesse the murder.

BAKER. Suer hee hath slayne him, for murder is confest.

D'AVER. 'Tis better still.

        Enter ASHBURNE, GODFREY, *etc.*

GODF. Was never knowne the lyke!

BAKER. Is Ritchard slayne? 45
I sawe Fryar Jhon, arm'd dreadfully with weapons
Not to bee worne in peace, pursue his lyfe;
All which I'l tell the abbott. [*Exit.*]

ASHB. Most strange it is that the pursude is fownd
To bee the murderer, the pursuer slayne. 50
How was it, Godfrey? Thou wast vpp beefore mee,
And canst discoorse it best.

GODF. Thus, syr: at noyse of murder, with the tramplinge
Of horse and ratlinge armor in the streetes,
The villadgers weare waken from theire sleepes; 55
Som gap't out of theire windowes, others venter'd
Out of theire doores; amongst which I was one
That was the formost, and saw Ritchard stopt
At a turninge lane, then overtooke by Jhon;
Who not him self alone, but even his horse 60
Backing the tother's beast, seem'd with his feete
To pawe him from his saddle. Att this assault
Friar Richard cryes, "Hold, hold, and haunt mee not,
For I confesse the murder!" Folke came in,
Fownd th' one i' th' sadle dead, tother sprallinge 65
Vpon the earthe alyve, still cryinge out
That hee had doon the murder.

48 [*Exit.*]] *Exit Baker. B.* 55 waken] wakend *B.*

D'AVERNE. Exellent still; withdrawe, for wee are safe.

[*Exeunt.*]

Enter the ABBOTT, *the* BAKER, FRYAR RICHARD, *prisoner and guarded, etc.*

ABBOT. These mischeifes I foretould; what's mallyce elsse
Then murder half committed? Though th' event   7[
Be allmost aboue apprehention strange,
Yet synce thyne owne confession pleades thee guilty,
Thou shalt have leagall tryall.

F. RICH. I confess
I was the malefactor and deserve
Th' extremity of lawe; but woonder much   7[
Howe hee in such a short tyme after death
Should purchase horse and weapons.

ABBOTT. Murder's a sinne
Which often is myraculously reveal'd.
Lett justyce question that; beare him to prison,
The tother to his grave.   8[

BAKER. Beinge so valiant after deathe, mee thinkes hee deserves the honor to bee buried lyke a knight in his compleate armor.

ABBOTT. These thinges shoold not bee trifled. Honest frends,
Retyre you to your homes; these are our chardge.   8[
Wee will acquaint our patron with this sadd
And dyre desaster; fyrst his counsell vse,
Next as wee maye our innocens excuse.   [*Exeunt.*]

68 [*Exeunt.*] *Om. B.*
Margin above 69 Stage-keepers as a guard. *MS.*

ACTUS QUINTUS

SCENA TERTIA ET VLTIMA

Enter MILDEWE *and* SARLABOIS.

MILDEW. May the disease of Naples, nowe turn'd Frensh,
Take bothe the judge and jurors! They have doom'd
The fayre Palestra from mee.

  SARLAB. So they had
Scribonia too, and mulcted vs beesydes,
But that in part they did comiserate   5
Our so greate losse by sea.

  MILDEW. This is the curse
Belonges to all vs bawdes: gentle and noble,
Even th' ouldest fornicator, will in private
Make happy vse of vs with hugges and brybes;
Butt lett them take vs at the publick bensh,   10
'Gainst consciens they will spitt at vs, and doome vs
Vnto the post and cart. Oh the corruptnes
Of these dissemblinge letchers!

  SARLAB. 'Tis well yet
You have reserved one virgin left for sale;
Of her make your best profitt.

  MILDEWE. A small stocke   15
To rayse a second fortune; yet com, frend,
Wee will go seeke her out.

         Enter GRIPUS, *the fisherman.*
  FISHER. No budgett to be com by; my ould mayster,

and SARLABOIS] *Scored through in MS.*
3-6 SARLAB. . . . sea.] *Marked for omission in MS.*
13-17 SARLAB. . . . out.] *Marked for omission in MS.*

Hee stands on consciens to deliver it
To the trew owner, but I thinke in consciens 20
To cheate mee and to keepe it to him selfe;
Which hee shall never doo, to prevent which
I'l openly proclayme it. Oh yes—

   If any vserer or base exacter,
   Any noble marchant or marchant's factor, 25
   Bee't marchant venterer or marchant tayler,
   Bee hee Mr. Pylot, botswayne or saylor—
    Enter GODFREY.

GODFREY. Hist, Gripus, hyst!

FISHER. Peace, fellowe Godfrey. I'l now play the blabber.
If eather passinger, owner, or swabber 30
That in the sea hathe lost a leather budget
And to the dolphins, whales, or sharkes doth grudge it—

GOD. Wilt thou beetraye all? I'l go tell my mayster.

FISHER. Yes, Godfrey, goe and tell him all and spare not;
I am growne desperate; if thou dost, I care not. 35

MILDEW. Hee talkt of a leatheren budgett lost at sea;
More of that newes would please mee.

FISHER. Bee hee a Cristian or beeleeve in Mawmett,
I such a one this night tooke in my drawnet.

MILDEW. My soone, my child, nay rather, thou yonge man, 40
I'l take thee for my father, for in this
Suer thou hast new beegott mee.

FISHER. Blessinge on thee!
But shoold I have a thousand children more,
I almost durst presume I never should have
Another more hard favored.

MILDEW. Thou art any thinge. 45
But hast thou such a budgett?

27 *Enter* GODFREY.] *Enter Godfrey to them.* MS. B. (to them *in later hand*).

FISHER. Syr, I have,
And new tooke from the sea. What wold'st thou giue
And have it sayfe?

MILDEW. I'l giue a hondred crownes.

FISHER. Tush, offer me a sowse but not on the eare;
I will barr that afore hand.

MILDEW. And all safe,   50
I'l giue thee then too hondred.

FISHER. Offer mee a cardeq!

MILDEW. Three hondred, 4, nay fyve
So nothinge bee deminisht.

FISHER. I will have
A thousand crowns or nothinge.

MILDEW. That growes deepe.

FISHER. Not so deepe as the sea was.

MILDEW. Make all safe,   55
And I will giue a thousand.

FISHER. 'Tis a match,
But thou wilt sweare to this.

MILDEW. Giue mee myne othe.

FISHER. If, when fyrst I shall behold
    My leatheren bagge that's stuft with gould,
    At sight thereof I pay not downe   60
    To Gripus every promist crowne—
       Now say after mee:
    May Mildewe, I, in my best age—

MILDEW. May Mildewe, I, in my best age—

FISHER. Dy in some spittle, stocks, or cage.   65

MILDEW. Dy in some spittle, stocks, or cage.

FISHER. I'l keepe my promisse; fayle not thou thine oathe.
So inn and tell my mayster.   [*Exit.*]

49 on the] in th' *B.*   68 *Exit.*]] [*Exit Fisherman. B.*

MILDEW. Yes, bawdes keepe oathes! 't must bee in leap-yeare
then,
Not now; what we sweare wee'l forsweare agen.   70
        Enter ASHBURNE, GODFREY, *and* GRIPUS.
ASHBURNE. And hee in that did well, for heaven defend
I shoold inritche mee with what's none of myne.
Where is the man that claymes it?
    GRIP. Heare's my sworne soon, that but even nowe acknowl-
edg'd mee to bee his father.   75
    ASHBURN. Knowest thou this?
    MILDEW. Yes, for myne owne. I had thought, lyke one for-
lorne,
All fort[u]ne had forsooke mee, but I see
My best dayes are to com. Welcom my lyfe!
Nay, if there be in any bawde a sowle,   80
This nowe hathe mett the body.
    ASHBURNE. All's theire safe,
Vnrifled, naye vntutcht, save a small caskett
With som few trifles of no valewe in't,
Yet to mee pretious, synce by them I have fownd
My one and only doughter.
    MILDEW. Howe's that, pray?   85
    ASHBURN. Thus: thy Palestra is my Mirable.
    MILDEW. Nowe may you to your comfort keepe the guirle,
Synce of my wealthe I am once againe possest.
I heare acquitt you of all chardges past
Due for her education.
    ASHB. You speake well.   90
    GRIP. It seemes you are possest, and this your owne.
    MILDEW. Which I'l knowe howe I part with.
    GRIP. Com quicly and vntrusse.

    70 GRIPUS.] *Gripus to 'em MS. B.* (to 'em *in later hand*).

MILDEW. Vntrusse, syr? what?

GRIP. Nay, if you stand on poynts, my crownes, my crownes;
Com tell them out, a thousand.

MILDEW. Thousand deathes   95
I will indure fyrst, synce I neather owe thee,
Nor will I paye thee, any thinge!

GRIP. Didst thou not swear?

MILDEW. I did, and will againe
If it bee to my profitt, but oathes made
Vnto our hurt wee are not bound to keepe.   100

ASHB. What's that you chalendge, Gripus.

GRIPUS. Not a sowse lesse
Then a full thousand crownes.

ASHBUR. On what condition?

GRIP. So much hee vowed and swore to paye mee down
At sight of this his budgett; a deneere
I will not bate; downe with my dust, thou perjur'd.   105

ASHBUR. But did hee sweare?

MILDEW. Suppose it; saye I did.

ASHBUR. Then thus I saye: oathes ta'ne advisedly
Ought to b[e kept]; and this I'l see perform'd.
What's forfet to my man is due to mee;
I claime it as my right. These your bawde's fallacyes   110
In this shall no waye helpe you. You shall answer it
Now as a subject and beefore the judge.

MILDEW. If I appeare in coort, I am lost againe;
Better to part with that then hazard all.
These bagges conteine fyve hondred pownds apeece,   115
Tak't and the pox to boot.

GRIP. And all these myne?

GODFREY. Woold I might have a share in't.

105 perjur'd] perjurer *B*.

ASHB. Nowe tell mee, Mildew, howe thou ratest the freedome
Of th' other virgin, yonge Scribonia,
Companion with my doughter?

MILDEW. I am weary　　　　　　　　　120
Of this lewde trade; giue mee fyve hondred crownes
And take her; I'l gee't over now in tyme
Ere it bringe mee to the gallowes.

ASHB. There's for her ransome; shee's from hencforthe free.

GRIP. Howe, syr?　　　　　　　　　125

ASHBURN. These other, Gripus, still beelonge to thee
Towards thy manumission.　　　　　[*Exit* GODFREY.]

Enter at one doore ISABEL, PALESTRA, SCRIBONIA;
at the other RAPHAEL, TREADWAY, THOM. ASHB.,
& the CLOWNE *aloofe.*

RAPHAEL. If all bee trewe my man related to mee,
I have no end of joy.

ASHBUR. This is my Mirable,
My doughter and freeborne; and if you still　　　130
Persist the same man you profest your self,
Beehold, shee is your wyfe.

RAPHAEL. You crowne my hopes.

MIRABL. This very day hathe made mee full amends
For many yeares of crosses.

TREADW. Nowe my suite.

RAPHAEL. Nor are my expectations yet at heighte　　　135
Before my frend bee equally made blest
In this fayer damsell's love.

TREADW. To accomplishe which,
If all the wealth that I injoye by land,
Or what at sea's in venter, will but purchase

127 thy] the *B.*　　　　127 [*Exit* GODFREY.]] *Om. B.*
127 ISABEL] *Om. B. Scored through in MS.*　aloofe] *Om. B.*

With her release a tye of love to mee,　　　140
This hower it shal be tender'd.

ASHB. Offer'd fayrely;
But knowe, syr, could you winne her to your wishes,
Shee shall not lyke a bondemayde come to ye;
Fyve hondred crownes are tender'd downe all redy
(Vnknowne to her) for her free liberty.　　　145

SCRIB. This is a jubeily, a yeare of joy,
For chastaty and spotles inocens.

TREADW. Shall I intreate you to receive them backe?
Lett it bee made my woorke of charity.

ASHB. I knowe you woorthy, but that must not bee;　　　150
Yet proove her, coort her, with my free consent,
And vse the best love's rethorick you can.
If with the motion shee rest satisfied,
And you pleas'd to accept her, it shall never
Be sayde you tooke a captyve to your bedd,　　　155
But a free woman.

TREADW. Nobly have you spoake.

RAPHAEL. Fayre Mirable, the fyrst thinge I intreate you
In which to expresse your love, speake for my frend.

MIRABLE. And with my best of oratory.

WYFE. Wee'l bee all
Assistants in the motion.

ASHBUR. If you prevayle,　　　160
I in the absens of some nearer frend
Have vow'd to stand her father.

CLOWNE. Nowe, sir, I have showed him you, but are you
ever the wyser?

THOMAS ASH. Peace, I am somwhat trobled. Oh 'tis hee,　　　165
My brother; and those rude and violent gusts

　159, 160 WYFE . . . motion.] *Scored through in MS.* WYFE] RAPH *B.*

That to this strange road thrust my shipp perforce,
And I but late for newe desasters curst,
Have with there light winges mo[u]nted mee aloft,
And for a haven in heaven new harbor'd mee.   170
Yet they but feede vpon theire knowne delights;
Anon I'l make them surfett.

   SCRIB. If to this frendly, fayer society,
I, a poore desolate virgin, so much bownd,
Should putt you off with delatory trifles   175
When you importune answer, t'wold appeare
In mee strange incivility: I am yours
And, beeinge so, therefore consequently his.

   ASHB. A match then! But, ere further you proceede,
Resolve mee one thinge, Mildewe,—not as thou art   180
Thy self, but as thou once weart made a Christian,—
Knowest thou this made's discent and parentadge?

   MILDEW. I will resolve you lyke a convertite,
Not as the man I was; I knew there byrths,
But for myne owne gayne kept them still conceal'd.   185

   ASHB. Now as thou hop'st of grace—

   MILDEW. The nurse, late dead,
That had these too in chardge, betrayde ashipboard
And ravisht from her coontry, ere she expyr'd,
Nam'd her the doughter of Jhon Ashburne, marcha[n]t.
Her I Palestra cal'd, shee Mirable;   190
That, Winefryde, doughter to Thomas Ashburne,
Brother to the sayde Jhon, I cal'd Scribonia.
They too are coosin germans.

   ASHB. This our neece?

   THOMAS. My doughter?

   PALESTRA. Partners in sorrowe, and so neere allyde,   195

   168 newe] *A correction in MS. for* strange.

And wee till nowe neare knewe it!

   SCRIB. My deere coosin.

   ASHBUR. Nay, I'l bee my woords' mayster; reache your
  hands,

And thoughe no nearer then an unkle, once

I'l playe the father's part.

   THOMAS. Praye hold your hand, sir;

Heare's one that will doo't for you.

   ASHBUR. Brother Thomas!   200

   THOMAS. Peruse that letter, whylst I breathe these joys,

Impartinge those a most vnlimitted love

In equall distribution. Doughter, neece,

Brother, and frends, lett mee devyde amongst you

A father's, brother's, and a kinsman's yoake,   205

With all th' vnmeasured pleasures and delights

That thought of man can wishe you.

   ASHBUR. Spare reply.

These tell mee that those bloodhownds who pursude

My fall, my oppressinge creditors I meane,

Are gone before to answer for my wronges,   210

And in there deathes with due acknowledgment

Of all theire violents doon mee; peace with them!

That lykewyse by the deathe of a ritche alderman,

My vnkle, I am left a fayer estate

In land, eight hondred by the yeare, in coyne   215

Twenty-fyve thousand pownd. Make mee, oh heaven,

For this greate blessinge gratefull! And not least

To you my indeer'd brother.

   THOMAS. One thinge woonders mee,

That I should fynd you neare Marcellis heare

When I was aym'd for Florens; where your letters   220

  201 joys] joy *MS.*

Inform'd mee you weare planted.

ASHB. But even thether

Those crewell men dog'd mee with such pursuit

That theire I fownd no safety, but was forĉt

To fly thence with that little I had left

And to retyre mee to this obscure place;   225

Where by the trade of fishinge I have lyv'd

Till nowe of a contented competens.

Those bates, hookes, lynes, and netts for thy good servyce,

Gripus, I nowe make thyne.

GRIP. You are my noble mayster, and wold I could have 230

fownd more tricks then these in my budgett; they had bin all

att your servyce.

ASHB. I purpose nowe for England, whether so please

These gentlemen consort vs with theire brydes.

BOATH. Most willingly.

ASHB. There you shall see what welcom   235

Our London, so much spoake of heare in France,

Can giue to woorthy strangers.

THOMAS. Att my chardge

Your shippinge is provyded, and at anchor

Lyes ready in the roade.

ASHBUR. Oh happy storme

That ends in such a calme!   240

Enter GODFREYE *in hast.*

GODFREY. Staye, gentlemen, and see a dolefull sight;

One ledd to execution for a murder

The lyke hath scarce bin heard of.

ASHBURNE. Of the fryar?

In part wee weare ey-witness of the faĉt,

Nor is our hast so greate but wee maye staye   245

To viewe his tragick end, whome the strickt lawe

Hathe made a just example.

    Enter the ABBOT, FRYAR RICHARD, SHREVE,
        and OFFICERS, *etc.*

  ABBOTT. Vpon thy trewe confession I have giuen thee
Such absolution as the churche allowes.
What hast thou elce to saye ere thou art made   250
To all men heare a wofull spectacle?

  FRYAR RICHARD. This only, that beetwixt Fryar Jhon
  and mee
Was ever hate and mallyce; and although
With no entent of murder, this my hand,
This most vnfort[u]nate hand, beereft his lyf,   255
For which vild deede I mercy begge of heaven;
Next of the woorld, whome I offended too,
Pardon and pitty. More to saye I have not:
Heaven, of my sowle take chardge, and of my body
Dispose thou, honest hangeman.   260

  CLOWNE. Lasse, poore fryar, and yet there's great hope of
his soule, for I canot spye one heyre beetwixt him & heaven.

  FISHER. And yet I dowbt hee will make but a bald reckninge
of it.

    Enter the L. DE AVERNE *and his man* DENNIS.

  AVERNE. Staye the execution.   265

  ABBOTT. Our noble fownder out of his greate charity
And woonted goodnes begg'd him a repreive!

  AVERNE. Brought a repreive I have: lett go the fryar,
And take from mee your warrant; I dischardge him.

  SHERIFF. And yet, my l[ord,] 'tis fitt for our dischardge   270
That the Kinge's hand bee seene.

  AVERNE. If not my woord
Will passe for currant, take my person then,

  247 *etc.*] *Om.* B.

Or if you thinke vnequall the exchange,
I tender my man's too to valew his.
Meane tyme dismisse him as one innocent   27⟨
Of what hee is condemde.

    ABBOTT. By his owne mouthe
Hee stands accus'd.

    AVERNE. And witnes all of you,
As freely I acquitt him.

    SHERIF. Honored syr,
Praye bee more plaine; wee vnderstand you not.

    AVERNE. I'l make it playne then.   28⟨

    CLOWN. Nowe, if thou beest wyse, drawe thy neck out of
the collar; doo, Slipp-stringe, doo.

    RICHARD. Marry, with all my hart, and thanke him too.

    AVERNE. Attend mee, reverend father, and you all
Of this assembly: for som spleene conceiv'd   28⟨
Against the fryar deceast, I strangled him,
The cause why, no man heare importun mee;
For manye reasons to my self best knowne
I hold fitt to conceale it, but I murdered him
In myne owne howse.

    ABBOTT. But by your honour's favour   29⟨
How can that bee when Richard heare confest
Hee slewe him in our cloyster?

    AVERNE. Heare me outt.
At fyrst, vntutcht with horror of the fact,
My purpose was to laye the guilt elswhear,
And for that purpose cause my man to mount him   29⟨
Over the cloyster wall.

    274 valew] *A correction in MS. for* equall.
    277 accus'd] *A correction in MS. for* condemde.
 · 295 cause] caus'd *B.*

DENNIS. Which soone I did
By th' helpe of a short ladder, sett him theire
In a close-place, and thoughe not of the sweetest,
Yet, as I thought, the safest; left him then.
   F. RITCH. Just in that place I fownd him, and imadgining   300
He satt of purpose theire to despight mee,
I hitt him with a stone; hee fell withall,
And I thought I had slayne him.
   DENNIS. But how the devill
Gott hee into our porche? That woonders mee.
   F. RICHARD. I fownd a ladder theire.
   DENNIS. The same I left.   305
   F. RICH. Gott him vpon my shoolders, and by that
Conveigh'd him back and left him in that porch,
Wheare, as it seemes, you fownd him.
   AVERNE. This troblinge vs, it drove vs to newe plotts.
Wee arm'd the fryar, accoutred as you sawe,   310
Mo[u]nted him on a stallion, lockt him fast
Into the saddle, turn'd him forthe the gates
To trye a second fortune.
   F. RICH. Just at the tyme
When, I beeinge mounted on the baker's mare,
The gates weare sett wyde ope for mee to fly.   315
   ABBOT. So that it seemes one beast pursuide the tother,
And not the dead Fryar Richard.
   AVERNE. Howsoevėr,
As one repentant for my rashnes past
And loathe to imbrewe mee in more innocent blood,
I fyrst confesse my servant's guilt and myne,   320
Acquitt the fryar, and yeild our persons vpp
To the full satisfaction of the lawe.

   299 then] there *B.*

Enter the LADY AVERNE *and her maid*, MILLESENT.

LADY. Which, noble sir, the Kinge thus mittigates;
See, I have heare your pardon. In the tyme
That you weare ceas'd with this deepe melancholly   325
And inward sorrowe for a sinne so fowle,
My self in person posted to the Kinge
(In progresse not farr off), to him related
The passadge of your busines, neather rose I
From off my knees till hee had sign'd to this.   330
    AVERNE. Th' hast doon the offyce of a noble wyfe.
His grace I'l not despyse, nor thy great love
Ever forgett, and if way maye bee fownd
To make least sati[s]faction to the dead,
I'l doo't in vowed repentance.
    ABBOT. Which our prayers   335
In all our best devotions shall assist.
    ASHBUR. All ours, great syr, to boote.
    AVERNE. Wee knowe you well and thanke you.
    ASHBURN. But must nowe
Forsake this place, which wee shall ever blesse
For the greate good that wee have fownd therein,   340
And hence remoove for England.
    AVERNE. Not beefore
All your successfull joyes wee heare related
To comfort our late sorrowes; to which purpose
Wee invite you and your frends to feast with vs.
That granted, wee will see you safe aboord;   345
And as wee heare rejoyce in your affayers,
Forgett not vs in England in your prayers.
                                [Exeunt.]
                        FINIS.

Notes.

NOTES

ACT I: SCENE I

THIS scene is an elaboration and dramatization of a portion of the *Prologue* of Plautus' *Rudens* (Bohn, pp. 66-67): "this Procurer brought the maiden hither to Cyrene. A certain Athenian youth, a citizen of this city, beheld her as she was going home from the music-school. He begins to love her; to the Procurer he comes; he purchases the damsel for himself at the price of thirty minæ, and gives him earnest, and binds *the Procurer* with an oath. This Procurer, just as befitted him, did not value at one straw his word, or what, on oath, he had said to the young man. He had a guest, a fit match for himself, an old man of Sicily, a rascal from Agrigentum, a traitor to his *native* city; this fellow began to extol the beauty of that maiden, and of the other damsels, too, that were belonging to him. *On this* he began to persuade the Procurer to go together with himself to Sicily; he said that there the men were given to pleasure; that there he might be enabled to become a wealthy man; that there was the greatest profit from courtesans. He prevails."

1.1.9. *The stayneles swanne With all the ocean's water canott wash The blacknes from her feete.* Possibly an adaptation of *Titus Andronicus,* 4. 2. 101:

> "For all the water in the ocean
> Can never turn the swan's black legs to white,
> Although she lave them hourly in the flood."

1.1.18. *Lais.* A famous courtesan of Corinth, born about 480 B.C., loved by Aristippus, Diogenes, and others. She is mentioned in *A Challenge for Beauty* (5. 1, p. 69) as a notable example of unchastity.

1.1.26. *vnbecom.* Queried by Bullen, but this is clearly the reading of the MS. The context shows that the word is used in the sense of "to deprive," a meaning that I have not found cited in the dictionaries.

1.1.61. *Neapolitan seignor.* A correction in the MS. for *French Monster, Seignior* also having replaced *Monsieur* in line 59 above. Bullen has *French monster, Neapolitan Seignor,* but obviously only the correction should be retained.

151

1.1.72 ff. *more leakinge vessayles*, etc. Bullen cites *I Edward IV*, p. 38: "Commend me to blacke *Luce*, bouncing *Bess*, and lusty *Kate*, and the other pretty morsels of man's flesh. Farewell, pink and pinnace, flibote and caruel, *Turnbull* and *Spittal!*"

1.1.75. *the huge greate baye of Portingall*. Wright (Furness' *As You Like It*, p. 225) says the expression *bay of Portugal* is "still used by sailors to denote that portion of the sea off the coast of Portugal from Oporto to the headland of Cintra. The water there is excessively deep, and within a distance of forty miles from the shore it attains a depth of upwards of 1400 fathoms, which in Shakespeare's time would be practically unfathomable."

1.1.102. *Sometymes by fayre means, then againe by force.* Bullen's *foul* for *force* seems more natural, but *force* is pretty clearly the MS. reading. Heywood contrasts "fair means" with "force" again in 4.1.111, 112.

1.1.122. *Mr. Mildewe. Mr.* has been changed in the MS. into what may be intended as an abbreviation for *Seignior*.

1.1.213. *these peevishe harletryes.* The expression "A peevish self-will'd harlotry" is twice used by Shakespeare, in *Romeo and Juliet*, 4.2.14 and again in *I Henry IV*, 3.1.199. White (quoted in Furness' *Romeo and Juliet*, p. 225) says: "This phrase was used with as little meaning of reproach in Elizabeth's time as 'slut' was in Queen Anne's."

ACT I: SCENE II

1.2.99. (*Y'are a rogue, Ritchard.*) This aside, like that in the next speech, is extra-metrical.

1.2.124-28. Cf. Masuccio, *Novel the First*, p. 17: "because it happened that the house of the lady was quite near to the convent, he began once more to cast his amorous glances upon her with such constant importunity, that she could not gaze out of a window, or go to church, or to any other place without doors, and not find the provoking monk continually hovering around."

ACT I: SCENE III

This scene is indebted, more or less completely, to *Rudens*. Lines 1-24 are an elaboration of *Rudens*, 1.1; lines 24-72 take the place of *Rudens*, 1.2, a very brief scene in which Plesidippus expresses to three citizens his determination to visit the Temple of Venus on the bare chance of discovering the Procurer; the rest of the scene (lines 73-168) is a free adaptation of *Rudens*, 1.3, 4. Passages that have been imitated most closely from Plautus will be noted below.

1.3.1-24. Cf. *Rudens*, 1.1:

"SCEPARNIO (*to himself*). O ye immortal Gods, what a *dreadful* tempest has Neptune sent us this last night! The storm has unroofed the cottage . . . ; it has so knocked all the tiles from off the roof; more light has it given us, and has added to our windows."

1.3.21. *King Agathocles.* Tyrant of Syracuse (361-289). Heywood was probably thinking, however, not of Agathocles, who was poisoned (Grote, *Hist. of Greece*, chap. 97), but of Pyrrhus, King of Epirus, who, as he fought at night in Argos, was struck on the head by an enormous tile, and falling from his horse, was killed by one of the soldiers of Antigonus.

1.3.77-83. Cf. *Rudens*, 1.3:

"PLESIDIPPUS. Health to you, good father, and to both of you, indeed.

DÆMONES. Health to you.

SCEPARNIO. (*to* PLESIDIPPUS, *who is muffled up in a coat*). But whether are you male or female, who are calling him father?

PLES. Why really, I'm a man.

DÆMONES. *Then*, man, go seek a father elsewhere. I once had an only daughter, that only one I lost. Of the male sex I never had a child."

1.3.84. *fort[u]nate*. Possibly better printed, here and elsewhere, *fort'nate*.

1.3.86-100. Cf. *Rudens*, 1.3:

"PLESIDIPPUS. Inform me on what I ask you; whether you have seen here any frizzle-headed fellow, with grey hair, a worthless, perjured, fawning knave.

DÆMONES. Full many a one; for by reason of fellows of that stamp am I living in misery."

1.3.116. *hunt dry foote*. An obsolete expression meaning to track game by the mere scent of the foot (*N.E.D.*).

1.3.142 ff. Plautus has the two women escape in a ship's boat; from this they are washed by the violence of the waves, but are fortunately then in such shallow water that they are able to wade to shore.

1.3.147. *I woold I weare som dolphin or some whayle That they might sitt astryde vpon my backe.* Cf. *Eng. Traveler*, 2.1, p. 29: "thinking to scape As did Arion, on the Dolphins backe."

ACT II: SCENE I

The first 74 lines of this scene are an adaptation of *Rudens*, Act I, Scenes 5 and 6.

2.1.1-20. Cf. *Rudens*, 1.5: "Do I receive this meed in return for my exemplary piety? For to me it would not prove a hardship to endure this laborious lot, if I had conducted myself undutifully towards my parents or the Gods; but if studiously I have exerted myself to beware *of that*, then, unduly *and* unjustly, Deities, you send upon me this. For what henceforth shall the glaringly impious receive, if after this fashion you pay honor to the guiltless? But if I knew that I or my parents had done anything wicked, now should I have grieved the less. But the wickedness of *this* master *of mine* is pressing hard upon me, his impiety is causing my woes; everything has he lost in the sea; these are the remains (*looking at her dress*) of his property."

2.1.16. This line is followed in the MS. by three cancelled lines, for a discussion of which *see* Introduction, p. 11.

2.1.60. *In my reserv'd Scribonia.* Bullen's *restored Scribonia* may seem preferable, but his reading is not supported by the MS. For *reserve* with the meaning "preserve," not unusual in Elizabethan English, cf. *Measure for Measure*, 5.1.472:

> "one in the prison,
> That should by private order else have died,
> I have reserv'd alive."

2.1.84. *Som sweete echo.* Echo songs and scenes were not uncommon in the Elizabethan drama (*see* Baskervill, *English Elements in Jonson's Early Comedy*, pp. 245, 246).

2.1.100. *& yet man is then these much more crewell.* For a similar idea, cf. Shakespeare's familiar "Blow, blow, thou winter wind" (*As You Like It*, 2.7.174).

2.1.195. *monthe's mind.* "A more or less playful synonym for mind." The "month's mind" was "the commemoration of a deceased person by the celebration of masses, etc., on a day one month from the day of his death" (*N.E.D.*).

2.1.197. *And rayse my fortunes many storyes hye.* Bullen reads *steepes* for *storyes.* Naturally this does not suit him, and he adds in a foot-note: "So the MS. But I am tempted to read, at Mr. Fleay's suggestion, 'steeples.'" *Storyes* seems to me clearly the reading of the MS.

ACT II: SCENE II

The 179 lines that constitute this scene are adapted more or less consistently from *Rudens*, Act II, Scenes 1-7. Every one of the seven scenes has its counterpart in *The Captives*, the order of the scenes and the persons speaking being the same. The dialogue, however, differs in detail considerably.

2.2.35. Cf. *Rudens*, 2.2; "Save you, thieves of the sea."

2.2.38-46. Cf. *Rudens*, 2.2:

"TRACHALIO. *Have you seen* any old fellow, bald on the forehead and snub-nosed, of big stature, pot-bellied, with eyebrows awry, a narrow forehead, a knave, the scorn of Gods and men, a scoundrel, one full of vile dishonesty and of iniquity, who had along with him two very pretty-looking young women?

FISHER. One who has been born with qualities and endowments of that sort, 'twere really fitter for him to resort to the executioner than to the Temple of Venus."

2.2.56. The MS. is torn and illegible at this point.

2.2.73-74. Cf. *Rudens*, 2.4: "if he has deceived Gods and men, he has *only* acted after the fashion of Procurers."

2.2.87. *Shipp-wrack by land.* An allusion to a story of Timæus of Tauromenium (see Athenaios, *Deipnosoph.* 2.5) concerning some young men who, overcome by wine, imagined themselves shipwrecked, though they were all the time safe in their own dwelling. The same story was employed in one of the most lively scenes of *The English Traveler* (2.1, pp. 28, 29). For conjectures as to Heywood's immediate source, *see* W. Bang and H. de Vocht, *Englische Studien*, 36.389-91.

2.2.99. Cf. *Rudens*, 2.4: "Perished through drinking, I suppose; Neptune last night invited him to deep potations."

2.2.102-105. Cf. *Rudens*, 2.4: "she's afflicting herself in mind for this, because the Procurer took away a casket from her which she had, and in which she kept that by which she might be enabled to recognize her parents; she fears that this has been lost."

2.2.116. Cf. *Rudens*, 2.5: "Who is it so furiously making an attack upon our door?"

2.2.126-128. Cf. *Rudens*, 2.5:

"AMPELISCA. Prithee, why do you make so much fuss about the water—*a thing* that *even* enemy affords to enemy?"

2.2.140. *Who ever lov'd that lov'd not att fyrst sight?* Bullen points out that this line is from Marlowe's *Hero and Leander* (line 176). Shakespeare quotes the same line in *As You Like It* (3.5.82).

2.2.142-161: Cf. *Rudens*, 2.6:

"AMPELISCA. What shall I say to the Priestess for having delayed here so long a time? . . . How, even still, in my wretchedness do I tremble, when with my eyes I look upon the sea. (*She looks towards the shore.*) But what, to my sorrow, do I see afar upon the shore? My master, the Procurer, and his Sicilian guest, both of whom wretched I supposed to have perished in the deep. Still does thus much more of evil survive for us than we had imagined. But why do I delay to run off into the Temple, and to tell Palæstra this, that we may take refuge at the altar before this scoundrel of a Procurer can come hither and seize us here? I'll betake myself away from this spot; for the necessity suddenly arises *for me to do so.*"

2.2.148. *Exit*, in a later hand, appears in the margin after this line. Perhaps it was the intention of the reviser to end the scene here.

2.2.162-179. Cf. *Rudens*, 2.7: "how heartily I did draw this. The well seemed much less deep than formerly. How entirely without exertion did I draw this up. . . . I'faith, I shall now set down this pitcher in the middle of the road. But yet, suppose any person should carry away from here this sacred pitcher of Venus, he would be causing me some trouble. I'faith, I'm afraid that this woman's laying a trap for me, that I may be caught with the sacred pitcher of Venus. In such case, with very good reason, the magistrate will be letting me die in prison, if any one shall see me holding this. For it's marked with the name; itself tells its own tale, whose property it is. . . . It must *then* be carried in-doors *by me.*"

ACT II: SCENE III

This scene follows rather freely *Rudens*, Act II, Scenes 8 and 9.

2.3.1,2. Cf. *Rudens*, 2.8:

"LABRAX. The person that chooses himself to be wretched and a beggar, let him trust himself and his life to Neptune."

2.3.6. *Why*, *thou of none. None* has been changed in the MS., apparently by a later hand, to *one.* Neither reading is very satisfactory.

2.3.11. Following this line, these two deleted lines, pronounced illegible by Bullen, appear in the MS.:

"A magazine of ritches, even those
By whome I ment to rayse a fortune by."

The repetition of *by* at the end of the second line would not offend an Elizabethan.
Cf. *Coriolanus*, 2.1.18: "In what enormity is Marcius poor in?" For other exam-
ples, *see* Abbott's *Shakespearean Grammar*, § 407. I have not restored these lines to
the text because the similarity of line 28 below to the second of the two lines sug-
gests that Heywood himself was responsible for their scoring through.

2.3.14-18. Cf. *Rudens*, 2.8:
"CHARMIDES. Troth, I'm far from being surprised if your ship has been wrecked,
which was carrying yourself, a villain, and your property villanously acquired."

2.3.31-33. Cf. *Rudens*, 2.8: "No hot liquor-shop at all for sure does he provide;
so salt and cold the potions that he prepares."

2.3.50. *hott bathes to sweet in*. For the cure of venereal diseases. Jests on this
practice are common in the Elizabethan drama.

2.3.56-58. Cf. *Rudens*, 2.8: "What whale, I wonder, has gobbled up my wallet, where all my gold and silver was packed up?"

2.3.87 ff. Doggerel not dissimilar to this appears in several of Heywood's plays
(*The Four Prentices*, *I Edward IV*, *A Woman Killed with Kindness*, and others).
It is to be hoped that an Elizabethan audience was able to appreciate it more than
a modern reader can.

2.3.103. Cf. *Rudens*, 2.9:
"LABRAX. How many are there?
SCEPARNIO. Just as many as you and I make."

ACT III: SCENE I

3.1.—*with her mayde*. The words *and page*, scored through, follow *mayde* in
the MS. Obviously the presence of a page would not be welcome at such an inter-
view as follows.

3.1.81. *See* Introduction, p. 23.

3.1.88. *in heaven*. As a substitute for these words, *elsewhere* has been written
in the margin by what appears to be a different hand.

3.1.121. *Provyde mee ho[r]ses. I will ryde.* A similar pretense of setting forth
upon a journey was more than once used by Heywood in previous plays to bring

about the dénouement (see *A Woman Killed with Kindness*, p. 133, and *The Wise Woman of Hogsdon*, 4.1, p. 337). Here, however, Heywood seems merely to be following Masuccio's tale (*see* Introduction, p. 20).

ACT III: SCENE II

This scene is an adaptation of *Rudens*, Act III, Scenes 2-9.

3.2.70. *silsepaereales*. The MS. at this point is fairly clear. This word is probably merely a high-sounding coinage of the clownish Godfrey, without specific meaning. Bullen queries it without comment.

3.2.85. Cf. *Rudens*, 3.5: "My own women, in fact, I shall drag away this instant from the altar by the hair, in spite of yourself, and Venus, and supreme Jove."

3.2.109-111. Cf. *Rudens*, 3.5:
"LABRAX. May I at least address these women?
DÆMONES. You may not."

3.2.115. *Stafford's lawe*. Punningly for a thrashing (*N.E.D.*).

3.2.124. *wee have too stringes to our bo[w]*. Already proverbial in 1546, when John Heywood printed his *Proverbs*.

3.2.128. *chancery or starr-chamber*. Chancery, the highest court of justice next to Parliament; Star-chamber, a court of civil and criminal jurisdiction at Westminster. Under James I and Charles I, the Star-chamber became an instrument of royal tyranny, though there is no reason to suppose that Heywood is using the term with any such implication here.

3.2.135. *too Frensh crownes and they so crack[t.]* The Elizabethans were very fond of this pun. Bald heads were often called French crowns (French *écu*), the implication being that the baldness was produced by the "French disease."

3.2.139. *Stafford*. See note on line 115.

3.2.140-151. Cf. *Rudens*, 3.7:
"PLESIDIPPUS. And did the Procurer attempt by force *and* violence to drag my mistress away from the altar of Venus?
TRACHALIO. Even so.
PLES. Why didn't you kill him on the instant?
TRACH. I hadn't a sword.
PLES. You should have taken either a stick or a stone."

TRACH. What! ought I to have pelted *this* most villanous fellow with stones like a dog?''

3.2.174-177. Cf. *Rudens*, 3.8:

''PLESIDIPPUS. Didn't you receive an earnest of me for *this* woman,... and carry her off from here?

LABRAX. I didn't carry her off.

PLES. Why do you deny it?

LAB. Troth now, because I put her on board ship; carry her off, unfortunately, I couldn't. For my part I told you that this day I would make my appearance at the Temple of Venus; have I swerved at all *from that?* Am I not there?''

3.2.230. *I have a curst wyfe at home. Curst* often meant ''cross'' or ''shrewish''; cf. Heywood's *Rape of Lucrece*, p. 169, and *A Midsummer-Night's Dream*, 3.2.299:

> '' *Helena.* I pray you, though you mock me, gentlemen,
> Let her not hurt me : I was never curst ;
> I have no gift at all in shrewishness. ''

ACT III: SCENE III

3.3.44-53. Cf. Masuccio, *Novel the First*, p.18: ''Whereupon a waiting girl appeared and conducted him, as if he had been a blind man, through the darkness into the hall, where he deemed that he would be joyfully received by the lady herself.''

3.3.57. *See* Introduction, p. 24.

3.3.88. [*Lett's remove itt*]*then.* The first three words of this passage are to me illegible. I adopt Bullen's reading with some misgiving, in the hope that thirty-five years ago the writing was a trifle less dim.

3.3.101. *Any thinge For a quiet lyfe.* Bartlett does not trace this proverb beyond the title of one of Middleton's plays.

3.3.106. *museinge.* Bullen reads *museings,* but adds the following foot-note: ''So I read at a venture. The MS. appears to give 'Inseinge.' ''

ACT IV: SCENE I

Though a large part of this scene is derived from *Rudens,* the opening speech (lines 1-11) finds no counterpart there. Lines 12-416 have their source in *Rudens,* Act IV, Scenes 2-7; here and there passages are expanded, but a great deal is omitted.

4.1.8. *they singe with no lesse sweetenes.* The mermaid was often confused with the siren of classical mythology; cf. *Comedy of Errors,* 3.2.45. *See* also Chaucer, *Nun's Priest's Tale* (lines 449-451):

"Chauntecleer so free
Song merier than the mermayde in the see,
—For Phisiologus seith sikerly."

4.1.24-40. Cf. *Rudens,* 4.2.

"GRIPUS. This have I found in the sea today; whatever's in it, it's something heavy that's in it; I think it's gold that's in it. And not a single person is there my confidant *in the matter.* Now, Gripus, this opportunity has befallen you, that the Prætor might make you a free man from among the multitude. Now, thus shall I do, this is my determination; I'll come to my master cleverly *and* cunningly, little by little I'll promise money for my freedom, that I may be free. Now, when I shall be free, then, in fine, I'll provide me land and houses *and* slaves: I'll carry on merchandise with large ships: among the grandees I shall be considered a grandee."

4.1.46. *What art thou, a shrimpe, a dogg-fyshe, or a poore Jhon? Poor John* was a name for the hake salted and dried for food, often a type of poor fare. All three of these names were sometimes applied contemptuously to persons.

4.1.50-52. Cf. *Rudens,* 4.3: "no fish have I, young man; don't you be supposing I have. Don't you see that I'm carrying my dripping net without the scaly race?"

4.1.53-55. Cf. *Rudens,* 4.3:

"TRACHALIO. I'faith, I'm not wishing for fish so much as I am in need of your conversation."

4.1.64-134. These lines are imitated closely from *Rudens,* Act 4, Scene 3:

"GRIPUS. I do give you my word; I'll be true *to you,* whoever you are.

TRACHALIO. Listen. I saw a person commit a theft; I knew the owner to whom that same *property* belonged. Afterwards I came myself to the thief, and I made him a proposal in these terms: 'I know *the person* on whom that theft was committed; now if you are ready to give me half, I'll not make a discovery to the owner.' He didn't even give me an answer. What is it fair should be given me out of it? Half, I trust you will say.

GRIP. Aye, even more; but unless he gives it you, I think it ought to be told to the owner.

TRACH. I'll act on your advice. Now give me your attention; for it is to yourself all this relates.

GRIP. What has been done *by me?*

TRACH. (*pointing to the wallet*). I've known the person for a long time to whom that wallet belongs.

GRIP. What do you mean?

TRACH. And in what manner it was lost.

GRIP. But I know in what manner it was found; and I know the person who found it, and who is now the owner. That, i'faith, is not a bit the more your matter than it is my own. I know the person to whom it now belongs; you, the person to whom it formerly belonged. This shall no individual get away from me; don't you be expecting *to get it* in a hurry.

TRACH. If the owner comes, shan't he get it away?

GRIP. That you mayn't be mistaken, no born person is there that's owner of this but my own self—who took this in my own fishing.

TRACH. Was it really so?

GRIP. Which fish in the sea will you say 'is my own'? When I catch them, if indeed I do catch them, they are my own; as my own I keep them. They are not claimed as having a right to freedom, nor does any person demand a share in them. In the market I sell them all openly as my own wares. Indeed, the sea is, surely, common to all persons.

TRACH. I agree to that; prithee, *then*, why any the less is it proper that this wallet should be common to me? It was found in the sea.

GRIP. Assuredly you are an outrageously impudent fellow; for if this is justice which you are saying, *then* fishermen would be ruined. Inasmuch as, the moment that the fish were exposed upon the stalls, no one would buy them; every person would be demanding his own share of the fish for himself; he would be saying that they were caught in the sea that was common *to all.*

TRACH. What do you say, you impudent *fellow?* Do you dare to compare a wallet with fish? Pray, does it appear to be the same thing?

GRIP. *The matter* doesn't lie in my power; when I've cast my hook and net *into the sea,* whatever has adhered I draw out. Whatever my net and hooks have got, that in especial is my own.

TRACH. Nay but, i'faith, it is not; if, indeed, you've fished up any article that's made.

GRIP. Philosopher, *you.*

TRACH. But look now, you conjurer, did you ever see a fisherman who caught a wallet-fish, or exposed one for sale in the market? . . . Of what color is it?

GRIP. (*looking at the wallet*). Of this color very few are caught: some are of a purple skin, there are great and black ones also. . . . If you are the helmsman of this ship, I'll be the pilot. Let go of the rope now, you villain. . . . Stay now; I've discovered by what method you may be neither thief nor sharer.

TRACH. By what method?

GRIP. Let me go away from here; you quietly go your own way, and don't you inform against me to any one, and I won't give anything to you. You hold your tongue; I'll be mum. This is the best and the fairest *plan.* . . .

TRACH. (*pointing to the cottage of Dæmones*). The person that lives in that cottage, should you like it to be decided by his arbitration?"

4.1.135-190. These lines have their source in a monologue by Dæmones which forms Aĉt 4, Scene 1, of *Rudens*, and in the following speeches from the beginning of Aĉt 4, Scene 4:

"DÆMONES (*to the Women*). Seriously, upon my faith, *young* women, although I wish what you desire, I'm afraid that on your account my wife will be turning me out of doors, who'll be saying that I've brought harlots here before her *very* eyes. Do you take refuge at the altar rather than I.

THE WOMEN. We, wretched creatures, are undone. (*They weep.*)"

4.1.192-194. Cf. *Rudens*, 4.3:
"GRIPUS (*aside*). By my troth, he never this day will award three obols away from his own servant."

4.1.199-214. Cf. *Rudens*, 4.4:
"TRACHALIO (*pointing to Gripus*). Is he your servant?

GRIPUS. I'm not ashamed *to say yes.*

TRACH. I've nothing to do with you.

GRIP. Then get you gone hence, will you.

TRACH. Prithee, do answer me, aged sir; is he your servant?

DÆMONES. He is mine.

TRACH. Oh then, that is very good, since he is yours. Again I salute you.

DÆM. And I you. Are you he who, not long since, went away from here to fetch his master?

TRACH. I am he.

DÆM. What now is it that you want?

TRACH. (*pointing to Gripus*). This is your servant, you say?

DÆM. He is mine.

TRACH. That is very good, since he is yours.

DÆM. What's the matter? . . .

TRACH. I fancy I'm to move the matter first.

GRIP. If indeed you were a decent person, you would be moving yourself off from here. . . . Will you give the right of speaking to a stranger sooner than to your own *servant?*"

4.1.200-203. These lines, as well as 209-213 below, are printed by Bullen as foot-notes. They follow the Latin play rather closely, and would seem to deserve to be included no less than other passages which, though scored through in the MS., were not relegated by Bullen to the position of foot-notes.

4.1.229. *all's not fishe that com's to nett*. Apparently a modification of the, at that time, familiar proverb, "All is fish that cometh to net" (quoted by John Heywood).

4.1.237. [*Enter Godfrey*.] Since Heywood has failed to indicate at what point between lines 190 and 241 Godfrey returns, I place his entrance arbitrarily at line 237.

4.1.244-250. Cf. *Rudens*, 4.4:

"GRIPUS. I'll trust it to you; but for you to return it me, if there are none of those things in it.

DÆMONES. It shall be returned.

GRIP. Take it."

4.1.268-284. Cf. *Rudens*, 4.4:

"PALÆSTRA. That is it. O my parents, here do I keep you locked up; here have I enclosed both my wealth and my hopes of recognizing you.

GRIPUS (*aside*). Then, by my faith, the Gods must be enraged with you, whoever you are, who fasten up your parents in so narrow a compass.

DÆMONES. Gripus, come hither, your cause is being tried. (*To Palæstra*.) Do you, young woman, away at a distance there say what's in it, and of what appearance; mention them all. By my troth, if you make ever so slight a mistake, even if afterwards you wish, madam, to correct yourself, you'll be making a great mistake."

4.1.318, 319. Cf. *Rudens*, 4.4:

"PALÆSTRA. There's also a golden drop, which my father presented to me upon my birthday."

4.1.344-362. Cf. *Rudens*, 4.7:

"DÆMONES. Tell him how this matter has fallen out about my daughter. Request him to leave other occupations and to come here.

TRACHALIO. Very well. DÆM. Tell him that I'll give him my daughter for a wife.

TRACH. Véry well. DÆM. And that I knew his father, and that he is a relation of my own.

TRACH. Very well. DÆM. But do make haste.

TRACH. Very well.

DÆM. Take care and let a dinner be prepared here at once.

TRACH. Very well. DÆM. What, all very well.

TRACH. Very well. But do you know what it is I want of you? That you'll remember what you promised, that this day I'm to be free.

DÆM. Very well. TRACH. Take care and entreat Plesidippus to give me my freedom.

DÆM. Very well. TRACH. And let your daughter request it; she'll easily prevail."

4.1.346 ff. *Ey, syr.* Heywood's rendering of Plautus' *licet.*

4.1.402-404. Cf. *Rudens*, 4.6:

"DÆMONES. What do I behold? Embracing her, my wife is clasping my daughter around her neck. Her caressing is *really* almost too foolish and sickening."

4.1.417. *Lett ech man speake as he's possest*, etc. In this song, Heywood follows the example of Greene, Lodge, and others, who were fond of praising rural life in the manner of Horace. Cf. Lodge's *Old Damon's Pastoral* and Greene's *Maesia's Song* and *The Shepherd's Wife's Song.*

ACT IV: SCENE II

4.2.9. *S. George a horsbacke.* St. George, the patron saint of England, was frequently represented, both on canvas and in stone, astride a mighty charger, with the dragon, newly slain, before him on the ground.

4.2.11. *Hee's where hee is in commons, wee dischardg'd.* The MS. shows that Heywood enlarged upon the idea contained in the first half of this line, and then, apparently reconsidering, crossed out what he had written. The passage originally ran thus:

"Hee's nowe where hee's in commons, wee. . .
Heare on this seate (nay hold your head vpp, Jhon,
Lyke a goodd boy), freely discharged our selfes," etc.

4.2.16 ff. The somewhat similar scene in *The Jew of Malta*, in which Friar Jacomo imagines he has killed Friar Barnardine (IV. 223), has been ascribed to Heywood. Besides the similarity of the two incidents, the fact that Heywood revived *The Jew of Malta* at court and at the Cock-pit, and published it in 1633 (no earlier edition is extant), lends the assumption some weight. P. Aronstein is inclined to attribute the passage to Heywood (*Anglia* 37. 255), but Professor C. F. T. Brooke considers that the relationship between the two scenes "cannot be held to prove that Heywood is author of the passage in *The Jew of Malta*, which is evidently earlier and less carefully worked out than the other version" (*Works of Christopher Marlowe*, p. 232). The probable currency of the old tale from which this incident is taken (*see* Introduction, p. 18) makes Heywood's responsibility for its occurrence in *The Jew of Malta* at any rate extremely doubtful.

4.2.26-33. Cf. Masuccio, *Novel the First*, p. 20: "God's faith, this fellow sits there, and refuses to make way for me, for no other reason than to show me, even in a matter of this sort, the enmity which he bears towards me through his ill will, but in this instance he will find his spite of no avail."

4.2.40. *See* Introduction, p. 24.

4.2.62. *Then I to tugge with benshes.* Dennis' speech originally ended thus:
"Then I to tugge with lawe. That done to secure
A guilty life and prevent deathe with shame,
By the same stepps returne the waye I came."
In the MS., *benshes* has been substituted for *lawe*, and the rest stricken through. Because of the similarity of these lines to lines 95 and 96 below, I have not restored them to the text. *See* Introduction, p. 12.

4.2.62-92. Cf. Masuccio, *Novel the First*, p. 22: "Messer Roderico, who all that night had slept little or not at all, through disquiet over the deed he had wrought, when at last the day was near at hand took occasion to send his servant into the purlieus of the convent, in order that by listening he might discover whether the friars had yet come upon the dead body of Maestro Diego, and what they might have to say about the matter."

4.2.92. *makes.* The subject of *makes* is "the presence of seditious thoughts." *See* Abbott's *Shakespearean Grammar*, § 337.

4.2.113. *On earthe to cry, "Vindicta!"* *See* the *Spanish Tragedy*, 3.13.1. This may, however, be a direct reference to Seneca's *Octavia: Vindicta debetur mihi.*

4.2. 133 ff. *See* Introduction, p. 21.

4.2.164. *mattens.* "One of the canonical hours of the breviary; properly a midnight office, but sometimes recited at daybreak" (*N.E.D.*).

ACT V: SCENE I

This scene is original with Heywood with the exception of lines 30-46, which have their source in *Rudens*, Act V, Scene I.

5.1. 30-40. Cf. *Rudens*, 5.1:

"PLESIDIPPUS. Has Palæstra found her father and mother?
TRACHALIO. She has found them.
PLES. And is she my countrywoman?
TRACH. So I think. PLES. And is she to marry me?
TRACH. So I suspect. PLES. Prithee, do you reckon that he will betroth her to me?"

5.1.70. *argentum potabile.* "A quibble on the *aurum potabile* of the old pharmacists." F. G. Fleay. "Aurum potabile, 'drinkable gold,' gold held in a state of minute subdivision in some volatile oil, formerly in repute as a cordial" (*N. E. D.*).

ACT V: SCENE II

5.2.12. *Least I shoold ryde another.* The word *mare* was humorously applied to the gallows.

5.2.22, 23. Cf. Masuccio, *Novel the First*, p. 23: "the stallion perceived by the odour he sniffed that a mare must be somewhere near about."

5.2.53-57. Cf. Masuccio, *Novel the First*, p. 24: "Now, because of this shouting and of the clatter made by the uncontrolled horses, all the townsfolk betook themselves to the doors and the windows—it being by this time broad daylight—and each one looked on in amazement."

ACT V: SCENE III

The first 127 lines of this scene are indebted to *Rudens*, most of the content of lines 1-17 being found in a brief monologue by Labrax that constitutes Act V, Scene 2, of *Rudens*, and lines 18-127 following, with considerable freedom, *Rudens*, Act V, Scenes 3 and 4. Lines 128-240 are original with Heywood (*see* Introduction, p. 16).

5.3.1. *the disease of Naples.* A form of syphilis. Italy shared with France, among Englishmen, the reputation of fostering and spreading venereal diseases.

5.3.2-13. Cf. *Rudens,* 5.2:

"LABRAX. Palæstra has just been taken from me by award. I'm ruined outright. But I do believe that Procurers were procreated for *mere* sport; so much do all persons make sport if any misfortune befalls a Procurer."

5.3. 18-27. Cf. *Rudens,* 5.3:

"GRIPUS. By my troth, in letters a cubit long, I'll immediately post it up in every quarter, 'If any person has lost a wallet with plenty of gold and silver, let him come to Gripus.' You shan't keep it as you are wishing."

5.3.47-70. Cf. *Rudens,* 5.3:

"GRIPUS. What would you be ready to give to one who should find these out for you, and give you information? Say speedily *and* at once.

LABRAX. Three hundred didrachms. GRIP. Rubbish.

LAB. Four hundred. GRIP. Old thrums.

LAB. Five hundred. GRIP. A rotten nut.

LAB. Six hundred.

GRIP. You are prating about mere tiny weevils. . . .

LAB. I'll give a thousand didrachms.

GRIP. You are dreaming. . . .

LAB. Say how much you ask.

GRIP. That you mayn't be adding anything against your inclination, a great talent; it's not possible for three obols to be bated thence; then do you say either 'yes' or 'no' at once. . . .

LAB. Be it so. GRIP. *(speaking, while Labrax repeats after him).* Venus of Cyrene, I invoke thee as my witness, if I shall find that wallet which I lost in the ship, safe with the gold and silver, and it shall come into my possession———. . .

LAB. *(to himself).* If ever so much he shall restore to me this wallet, I'm not this day indebted to him three obols even. It's according to my own intention what my tongue swears."

5.3.81-85. Cf. *Rudens,* 5.4:

"DÆMONES. Everything in it is safe; there has only been one casket taken out of it, with some trinkets, by means of which this day I have found my daughter."

5.3.89, 90. *I heare acquitt you of all chardges past Due for her education.* The procurer *(leno)* of classical times was accustomed to purchase young female slaves. Before selling them or letting them out as prostitutes, he would give them an excellent education. Indeed it is on her return from a music school that Palæstra, according to Plautus, is seen and loved by Plesidippus.

5.3.91-100. Cf. *Rudens*, 5.4:

"GRIPUS. Hark you, you've got the wallet now.

LABRAX. I have got it. GRIP. Make haste.

LAB. Make haste about what? GRIP. To pay me the money.

LAB. By my troth, I'll neither give you anything nor do I owe you anything. GRIP. What mode of proceeding is this? Don't you owe it me?

LAB. Troth, not I indeed. GRIP. Didn't you promise it me upon your oath?

LAB. I did take an oath, and now I'll take an oath, if it is in any way my own pleasure; oaths were invented for preserving property, not for losing it."

5.3.118-127. Cf. *Rudens*, 5.4:

"DÆMONES. Tell me, at what price did you buy that other young woman, Ampelisca?

LABRAX. I paid down a thousand didrachms.

DÆM. Should you like me to make you a handsome offer?

LAB. I should like it much. DÆM. I'll divide the talent.

LAB. You act fairly.

DÆM. For that other woman, *Ampelisca*, that she may be free, take you one half, *and* give the other half to him.

LAB. By all means.

DÆM. For that half I'll give his freedom to Gripus, by means of whom you found your wallet, and I my daughter."

5.3.127. [*Exit Godfrey.*] As Heywood has apparently forgotten to have Godfrey leave the stage in preparation for his return at line 240, I have placed his exit arbitrarily at this point.

5.3.281. *drawe thy neck out of the collar*. Perhaps proverbial. Cf. *Romeo and Juliet*, 1.1.4: "Ay, while you live, draw your neck out o' the collar."

Glossary.

GLOSSARY

THOUGH various dictionaries and lexicons have been consulted in the preparation of this glossary, *The New English Dictionary* has been my chief resource.

Agree, v. †Combine to prove (use not found in *N. E. D.*). 4.1.328.

Angle, n. Line and rod. *Arch.* 2.2.112.

Anticke, a. Grotesque. 1.2.63.

Arch-piller, n. †Worst of robbers. 3.2.107.

†Arrant, n. Errand. 4.1.366.

Ballanst, ppl. a. Steadied by reefing with a balance-reef. Possibly ballasted, loaded. 1.1.73.

†Basse [base], n. "A plaited skirt . . . ; also an imitation of this in mailed armor." *N. E. D.* 4.2.136.

Beaver, n. *Obs. exc. hist.* "The lower portion of the face-guard of a helmet, when worn with a visor." Planché. 4.2.138.

Brable, v. *Obs. or arch. exc. dial.* Dispute captiously. 4.1.6.

Budget, n. †A leather wallet or bag. 2.1.24.

Burn, v. †Infect with venereal disease. 2.3.30.

But, conj. If not, unless. *Arch.* 4.2.116.

Cage, n. †"A prison for petty malefactors." Johnson. 5.3.65.

†Cap-case, n. A traveling case, bag, or wallet. 4.1.74.

Capp a pe, adv. From head to foot. 4.2.144.

†Cardeq, n. "An old French silver coin worth ¼ of the gold *écu*." *N. E. D.* 5.1.69.

Cast, ppl. a. Discarded 4.2.131.

Catamiting, ppl. a. Keeping a boy for unnatural purposes. 2.2.97.

†Cater, n. A buyer of "cates," or provisions. 4.1.53.

Caudell, n. "A warm drink consisting of thin gruel, mixed with wine or ale, sweetened and spiced, given chiefly to sick people." *N. E. D.* 2.3.108.

†Cautelous, a. Cautious. 1.2.42.

Cease, v. Form of *seize*. 3.3.66.

Censure, n. †A judicial sentence. 3.2.209.

Close-place, n. A privy. 5.3.298.

Colt's toothe, n. Inclination to wantonness. 4.1.171.

†Combustious, a. Turbulent. 5.1.2.

Commons, n. †A privy. 4.2.11.

Condition'd, ppl. a. *Condition'd with:* in the control of, subject to the terms and conditions of. 1.1.101.

Congar [conger], n. A sea-eel. 4.1.42.

Congee, v. *Arch.* Bow. 1.2.122.

†Consequent, n. Logical inference. 1.1.5.

Consort, v. †Attend. 5.3.234.

Contentment, n. †Gratification. 3.3.43.

Convertite, n. *Arch.* A professed convert to a religious faith. 5.3.183.

Coole, n. Form of *cowl.* 5.2.14.

Copy-hold, n. An estate held by a kind of tenure in England of ancient origin called "copyhold." 4.1.93.

Cousininge, ppl. a. [A form of *cozening.*] Cheating, fraudulent. 1.3.94.

†Covent, n. An old form of *convent.* 1.2.7.

Coyle, n. Fuss, "row," confusion. 3.2.44.

Cras'd, ppl. a. [Form of *crazed.*] Diseased, infirm. 1.2.57.

Curst, ppl. a. Cross. *Obs. or arch.* 3.2.230; 4.1.186.

Damosella, n. [Form of *damosel.*] A young unmarried lady. 2.2.162.

Dauber, n. †A plasterer or builder of walls. 1.3.18.

Deathe's-man, n. *Arch.* A man who puts another to death. 3.3.120.

Deneere, n. [Form of *denier.*] "A French coin, . . . used as the type of a very small sum." *N.E.D.* 4.1.266.

Despight, v. †Vex or provoke to anger; spite. 5.3.301.

Discoorse, v. Relate. *Arch.* 5.2.52.

†Disguest, v. Digest. 4.1.437.

†Dispence, n. Dispensation; pardon. 3.2.60.

Dorser, n. A basket carried on the back, a pannier. 4.1.100.

Doubtfull, a. †Giving cause for apprehensions. 3.1.113.

Dowbt, v. Suspect. *Arch.* 1.1.107.

Dowbt, n. †Difficulty. 2.1.206.

Equll [equal], a. Impartial. 4.1.429.

Fact, n. †Performance, deed, action. 3.1.85.

Factor, n. Steward. 5.1. (opening stage directions).

Fallacy, n. †Deception, trick. 3.1.116; 5.3.110.

†False, v. Play false to, deceive. 2.1.12.

Fayre, adv. *Speake fayre:* address courteously. 4.1.34.

Fee-simple, n. "An estate in land, etc. belonging to the owner and his heirs forever." *N.E.D.* 4.1.93.

Fend, v. *Fendinge and proovinge:* arguing and wrangling. 4.1.3.

Fisguigge, n. [Form of *fisgig.*] A kind of harpoon. 4.1.31.

Flapp, n. Something broad with which to strike flies. 1.1.118.

Fly-boat, n. †A fast sailing boat. 1.1.74.

Fore-topp, n. †The lock of hair on the forepart of the crown. Fig. especially in phrase: *to take time by the fore-top.* 3.3.35.

Fraught, n. †Burden. 2.3.19.

Gally-foyst, n. *Obs. exc. hist.* "A state barge, esp. that of the Lord Mayor of London." *N.E.D.* 1.1.159.

Grizell, n. A meek and patient wife (from the name of Chaucer's heroine in the *Clerk's Tale*). 4.1.138.

Guarded, ppl. a. Trimmed, as with braid, lace, velvet. *Obs. exc. hist.* 3.2.179.

Harbor, n. Place of shelter or refuge. *Obs. exc. dial.* 2.1.37.

Harletrye, n. Harlot. 2.1.195.

Heyre, n. [Form of *hair.*] †Kind, quality. 1.3.36.

Impart, v. †Share. 3.1.55.

†Insidiate, v. Lie in wait for; plot against. 4.2.42.

Intendement, n. †Purpose. 3.1.79.

Intreate, v. *Obs. or arch.* form of *entreat.* 3.2.223.

†Intyre, v. [Form of *entire.*] Attach closely, endear. 1.1.55; 5.1.84.

Irreproovable, a. Undeserving of reproof. *Now rare.* 3.1.95.

Jack, n. "In the virginal . . . : An upright piece of wood fixed to the back of the key-lever, and fitted with a quill which plucked the string as the jack rose on the key's being pressed down." *N.E.D.* 2.3.52.

Jack sauce, n. A saucy fellow. 1.2.104.

Limitt, v. †Allot. 3.3.113.

Magazine, n. (1) †Stock of clothing. 2.3.41. (2) A place where goods are laid up. *Now rare.* 3.2.19.

†Makareele, n. A bawd. 4.1.158.

†Mangy, n. *Obs.* form of *mange.* 2.3.40.

Marry, int. *Obs. exc. arch. or dial.* ═Why to be sure. 4.2.164.

Mawmett, n. *Obs. exc. arch. and dial.* Used erroneously for *Mahomet.* 5.3.38.

†Mechall, a. (Only in Heywood.) Adulterous. 2.2.153.

Milt, n. The roe or spawn of the male fish. 4.1.104.

Misreated, ppl. a. *Now rare.* Misjudged. 1.1.169.

Motion, n. †Proposal. 5.3.153.

Mr., n. †An abbreviation of *Master.* 1.1.122.

†Mumbudgett, a. Silent. 4.1.124.

Murreine, n. [Form of *murrain.*] †Plague. 1.1.198.

Of, prep. †On. 4.1.366; 5.2.13; 5.3.227.

Opposite, a. †Hostile, antagonistic. 1.2.16.

Ordinarye, n. A tavern where public meals were provided at a fixed price. 1.3.59.

Owe, v. †Own. 4.1.75.

Patronadge, n. Protectorship. 3.2.218.

†Patronadge, v. Protect, defend. 3.2.12.

Patronise, v. †Secure protection for (use not noted in *N.E.D.*). 3.2.193.

Pox, n. †Syphilis. 5.3.116.

Peach, v. Inform against. *Now rare.* 4.1.70.

Peeterman, n. A fisherman (in allusion to the occupation of Simon Peter). 4.1.64.

Perewinkle, n. A kind of sea-snail. †Playfully applied to a girl or woman. 2.2.54.

Pink, n. A small sailing vessel. 1.1.73.

Plash, n. Puddle. 2.2.90.

Poynt, n. A cord for attaching the hose to the doublet. *Now arch. or hist.* 5.3.94.

Praune, n. A kind of shell-fish common off the coasts of Great Britain, and used as food. 2.2.14.

Progresse, n. A state journey. *Now somewhat archaic.* 5.3.328.

Proper, a. †Own. 1.1.212.

Punke, n. *Obs. or rare arch.* A prostitute. 1.1.73.

Purpose, v. †Be bound. 5.3.233.

Quaint, a. †Clever, full of fancies or conceits. 2.1.201.

Quale, v. [Form of *quell.*] Kill. *Now rare or obs.* 3.1.148.

Quest, v. ? Visit (an expression used of hunting dogs implying *to search about*). 1.1.142.

Rack, n. Clouds driven before the wind in the upper air. 1.3.43.

†Reguard, v. To guard doubly. 3.2.179.

Repayer, n. †Return. 1.3.63.

Repur'd, ppl. a. *Rare.* Purified again. 1.1.39.

Reserve, v. To save from death. *Now rare.* 2.1.60.

Rott, n. In the imprecation: *rott on.* 2.2.70.

Seralia, n. [Form of *seraglio.*] Harem. 3.2.71.

Shoone, v. [Form of *shun.*] Escape. *Now rare or obs.* 2.1.44.

Shreve, n. Form of *sheriff*. 5.3.247.

†Slipp-stringe, n. One who has shaken off restraint, a prodigal. 5.3.282.

Sollicite, v. Disturb. 4.2.85.

Sowse, n. A sou (Fr.); a blow. 5.3.49.

Speede, v. Kill. *Arch.* 5.2.39.

†Spittle, n. A hospital. 2.3.54.

Squetche, v. [Squitch.] *Now dial.* †Flinch or wince, fidget. 3.2.120.

Stagger, v. Hesitate. 1.1.82.

†Start-hole, n. Refuge, hiding-place. 1.3.115.

Still, adv. Always. 3.3.105.

Submisse, a. Submissive. *Obs. exc. arch.* 1.2.96.

Supplanting, n. †Causing the downfall of someone. 1.2.12.

†Suspeȼt, n. Suspicion. 3.3.123.

Swabber, n. One whose office it was to clean the deck of a vessel. 5.3.30.

†Syr-reverens, n. [Same as *saving your reverence*.] Used as apology for an impropriety in one's conversation, and later identified with the impropriety itself; *sir-reverens like:* base 3.1.12.

Temprature, n. Temperament. 1.1.93.

Tent, v. Probe. 1.3.48.

Testat, n. †Witness, testimony. 3.2.173; 4.2.41.

†Then, conj. Than. 3.2.117.

Too, prep. *Obs.* form of *to*. 3.3.70.

Too, adj. *Obs.* form of *two*. 3.1.133.

Toonne, n. [Form of *tun*.] A large cask for holding wine, etc. 1.3.92.

Topp-gallant, n. The top-gallant mast of a ship. 3.3.36.

Trewe, a. Honest. 2.2.37.

Trick, n. Knickknack. 5.3.231.

Vent, n. Market. 1.1.227.

Venter, n. *Obs.* form of *venture*. 3.3.132.

†Vild, a. A corrupt form of *vile*. 5.3.256.

Virginall, n. A spinet or small harpsichord. 2.3.52.

Vnbecom, v. ?Deprive. 1.1.26.

†Vnfallid, a. Infallible. 4.1.379.

Vnredy, a. † Not dressed. 4.2.96.

Vntrusse, v. Untie, unfasten. 5.3.93.

Whenas, conj. †When. 2.2.165.

†Whytinge mopp, n. A young whiting (fish); figuratively, a pretty girl. 2.2.170.

Widging, n. A wild duck. †A fool. 2.3.3.

Woonder, v. Amaze, surprise. *Rare.* 5.3.218.

Bibliography.

BIBLIOGRAPHY

Abbott, E. A. A Shakespearean Grammar. London, 1897.

Adams, J. Q. (Ed.) The Dramatic Records of Sir Henry Herbert. New Haven, 1917.

Aronstein, Philipp. "Thomas Heywood." Anglia. Vol. 37 (New Series, Vol. 25). Halle, 1913.

Baskervill, C. R. English Elements in Jonson's Early Comedy. (Bulletin of the University of Texas, April 8, 1911.)

Bédier, Joseph. Les Fabliaux. 2d edition. Paris, 1895.

Bullen, A. H. A Collection of Old English Plays. Vol. 4. London, 1885.

Cambridge History of English Literature. Vols. 5 and 6. (The Drama to 1642.) New York and Cambridge, 1910.

D., A. D. S. Les Comptes dv Monde Adventvrevx. (Ed. by Félix Frank.) 2 vols. Paris, 1878.

Fleay, F. G. A Biographical Chronicle of the English Drama, 1559-1642. London, 1891.

Fleay, F. G. A Chronicle History of the London Stage, 1559-1642. London, 1890.

Gilbert, A. H. "Thomas Heywood's Debt to Plautus." Journal of English and Germanic Philology. Vol. 12. 1913.

Hazlitt, W. C. (Ed.) Remains of the Early Popular Poetry of England. Vol. 3. London, 1866.

Heywood, Thomas. The Dramatic Works of Thomas Heywood, now first collected with Illustrative Notes and a Memoir of the Author. 6 vols. London, 1874.

Heywood, Thomas. Γυναικεῖον or Nine Bookes of Various History, concerninge Women, inscribed by the names of the Nine Muses. 1624. Rptd. as The General History of Women, 1657.

Kittredge, G. L. "Notes on Elizabethan Plays." Journal of Germanic Philology. Vol. 2. 1898.

Koeppel, Emil. "Zur Quellenkunde des Stuart-Dramas." Archiv für das Studium der Neueren Sprachen und Litteraturen. Vol. 97. Braunschweig, 1896.

Masuccio di Salerno. The Novellino of Masuccio. (Trans. by W. G. Waters.) London, 1895.

Montaiglon, Anatole de, et Raynaud, Gaston. Recueil Général et Complet des Fabliaux des xiiie et xive Siècles. 6 vols. Paris, 1872-90.

Murray, J. T. English Dramatic Companies, 1558-1642. 2 vols. London, 1910.

Plautus, Titus Maccius. The Comedies of Plautus. (Trans. by H. T. Riley.) London, 1894.

Schelling, F. E. Elizabethan Drama, 1558-1642. 2 vols. Boston and New York, 1908.

Taylor, A. "Dane Hew, Munk of Leicestre." Modern Philology. Vol. 15. 1917-1918.

Ward, A. W. A History of English Dramatic Literature to the Death of Queen Anne. 3 vols. London and New York, 1899.